GREY ZONE GOVERNANCE IN GEOPOLITICS

The Case of Artificial Intelligence

GREY ZONE GOVERNANCE IN GEOPOLITICS

The Case of Artificial Intelligence

PS Suryanarayana

KW Publishers Pvt Ltd
New Delhi

Indian Council of World Affairs
New Delhi

ISBN 978-81-975190-5-5 Hardback

Published in India by Kalpana Shukla

KW Publishers Pvt Ltd
4676/21, First Floor, Ansari Road
Daryaganj, New Delhi 110 002
Phone: +91 11 43528107
Marketing: kw@kwpub.in
Editorial: production@kwpub.in
Website: www.kwpub.in

Printed and bound in India

Contents

Foreword

Tech-India has the capability to steer the upcoming debates at the United Nations towards a fair global order for harnessing critical and emerging technologies. This is especially true of Delhi's potential for a key role in the rapidly advancing domain of artificial intelligence (AI). Significantly, as Prime Minister Narendra Modi emphasised in March 2024, the 'India AI Mission' is designed to make the country "a global leader in AI innovation".

In many ways, AI is gradually emerging as a unique game-changer in the lives and politics of people and nations. From the dawn of civilisation, innovations and inventions have often generated development opportunities, causing societal challenges. Nuclear technology, the most notable product of human ingenuity prior to the current debate on AI, became a source of 'clean energy' besides enabling weapons of mass destruction.

AI seems different in two ways. Its economic benefits of super-fast computerised operations have also led to concerns about real and potential job losses, etc. Secondly, the perceived 'autonomous' potential of 'Frontier AI' to cause unprecedented devastation is spreading fear that human control over this technology may be lost.

AI may be addressed during the UN Summit of the Future and beyond this gathering of world leaders in September 2024. While the UN has a vast array of political, economic and social issues to deal with, technology is increasingly becoming a core item on the global agenda. Cybersecurity, as well as the digital divide within and between countries, has been addressed for some time. However, AI has really come to the fore as a global attention-grabber.

In this timely monograph, PS Suryanarayana argues that a pathway to a global AI order is possible through geopolitical reform of the UN Security Council as the first step. A global AI order is necessary, in his view, because the highly advanced tech domains are 'grey zones' with little or no effective governance at this stage. I am sure the readers would find the monograph useful in understanding the debate around AI governance and geopolitics.

Amb. **Vijay Thakur Singh**
(Director General, ICWA)

July 19, 2024

Preface

As a technological marvel, Artificial Intelligence (AI) seems to propel the competitive quest for power among states in new ways. Non-state actors, too, aspire for AI-catalysed power to shape life and work. Almost universal is the perception of this hyper-technology's peerless potential for causing good and bad. As an innovation, AI has indeed been around for several decades. However, its impact on various aspects of our existence on Earth – from mundane daily chores to military might – has been felt strongly in recent years. The impact has been mind-boggling and even soul-stirring, serving as a wake-up call for states and others to administer the harnessing of AI at all geopolitical levels.

Punditry has traced the new awareness about AI to its rise and rise due to the dramatic qualitative increase in the computing power that fuels this hyper-tech system. Another reason is said to be the expanding availability of all categories of data, such as the feedstock for AI models. After getting trained first, every AI model/system embarks on its own guided or autonomous journey in the service of humanity or as its developer's weapon of choice.

A brief introductory case study of the efforts at global governance of AI is traced in this policy-relevant monograph. The study is based on this author's own recent research, as well as interviews and conversations with diplomats and other officials of several countries over a number of years.

Two South Indian sages – Tiruvalluvar and Tyagaraja – have, respectively, projected diplomacy as the art of speech and action that fits the trend of the times. While Tiruvalluvar communicated in Tamil, Tyagaraja (Kakarla Tyagabrahmam) composed his thoughts on celestial power-play in Telugu as an idiom of people on Earth. Similar perceptions about diplomacy abound in all other Indian languages too. In many ways, the trend of the times today can be described as techno-diplomacy or 'techplomacy'. These terms mean inter-state interactions driven by the high-tech capabilities of the countries concerned. This monograph is about the techplomacy that could help shape the global governance of AI going forward.

This author thanks the Indian Council of World Affairs (ICWA) and its Director-General, Her Excellency Vijay Thakur Singh, for the opportunity to discern today's techplomacy and write this monograph. It is timed for publication on the eve of the UN Summit of the Future in September 2024. Even beyond this signature event of the UN, this geopolitical case study of AI will be relevant to the readers and policy makers.

While thanking the reviewer of my manuscript for commending it, with modesty, I dedicate this brief introductory monograph to my generation and future generations all over the world. May hyper-technologies be used for the common good!

PS Suryanarayana
July 11 2024

Glossary

AD3: Advanced Domains Defence Dialogue. This dialogue, still in its early stage, covers the possibilities of US-India cooperation in advanced high-tech domains, including artificial intelligence.

AI: Artificial Intelligence. The simulation of human intelligence through computer science.

AI Arms (also, AI weapons, military AI): War-fighting and/or war-deterring weapons (including drones, etc.) powered by AI.

AI divide: A term for the gap between countries and/or entities in their respective capabilities in the rapidly advancing field of AI.

AI-LAWS: AI-powered Lethal Autonomous Weapons Systems (LAWS). It is a self-learning system (or model) of AI that enables a pilotless drone to select targets and kill them. The AI-powered drone can do this without being guided by the state or non-state actor concerned. This aspect might help the relevant state(s) or non-state actor(s) to disclaim responsibility for such killings in a war or other situations. The international debate on AI-LAWS is still evolving.

AI model/AI system: The AI model simulates human intelligence, especially the ability to see patterns in a situation, solve problems, make decisions, etc. The AI system includes the AI model and the required inputs like data, etc., as organised by the developer concerned.

AI race: The competition, mainly between two states or two coalitions of states, in the development, deployment and use of systems (or models) of AI. This applies to both civil and military purposes.

AI-savvy: Countries (and other actors) with the flair and expertise for research and development in the civil and military applications of AI.

AI superpower: A state believed to be far ahead of all (or most) other states in the realm of civil and military AI. Debatable is the belief in some quarters that the US and China are today's AI superpowers.

Algorithm: A software programme, often designed with sequential commands or rules, for computer(s) or robot(s) to produce desired results or outcomes. In the field of AI, algorithms are used to 'automate' decision-making in a simulation of human intelligence.

Arms race in cyberspace: A term that describes the computer-aided competition, mainly between two states or two coalitions of states, to disable (fully or partially) their respective adversary's military capabilities. In the virtual environment of the internet, such competition is driven by stealth operations. These are based on sophisticated intrusion into the adversary's military-use computers and/or computerised military signals.

Autonomy (with reference to AI systems): An AI system or model which can (or does) function independently of its developer (a state or non-state actor) is deemed to possess autonomy. The AI model/system does so through 'self-learning'. At first, each AI model is trained by its developer. Relevant data from various sources are used for this purpose. A 'trained' AI model/system becomes autonomous by 'learning' more from the data and by 'thinking' on its own.

BRF (also BRI): Belt and Road Forum. It was launched by Chinese President Xi Jinping in Beijing in May 2017. BRF is based on the Belt and Road Initiative (BRI). It is a platform to establish worldwide connectivity radiating out of China. Under BRI as a policy, Chinese-funded infrastructure projects, ranging from energy to strategic ports and airports, are built in China's partner countries. Through these means, Beijing has been seeking to create a worldwide web of China-friendly countries.

Baseline: Originally a sports terminology, it is used to denote a foundation or a starting point for principles, agreements, etc.

Bletchley Declaration: This document highlights the importance of safe frontier AI. It was adopted by 29 countries on November 1, 2023. India, the United States of America, China and the United Kingdom were among the signatories.

Borderless AI: This term signifies the reality that the development and use of AI is not the monopoly of one country or one coalition of countries. Individual states do try to preserve their respective 'AI secrets', especially in the military domain. However, AI technology – a product of the human mind – can be developed by any person anywhere. As a result, an AI system (or model) is not necessarily confined to the political boundaries of its state of origin.

CCW: Convention on Certain Conventional Weapons. It is a multilateral disarmament treaty adopted by the UN in 1980.

CPEC: China-Pakistan Economic Corridor, which Xi Jinping is proactively promoting. The corridor – a series of China's BRI projects – involves the presence of Chinese institutions and personnel in some disputed areas. Pakistan controls these areas, but India claims them as its sovereign territory. For this historical reason, India remains a conscientious critic of CPEC.

Calculus of power: In this monograph, the term denotes the approach or means by which a state or a coalition of states seeks to assert its respective rights in international relations. Such assertion is often backed by military strength. In other contexts, the term is suitably used in national politics with reference to various contenders for power.

Cascading AI wave: This is a metaphorical description of substantial developments in AI, one wave of progress succeeding another and so on.

Chinese characteristics: This is a term China uses to describe its 'unique' capabilities and achievements in almost all fields of human endeavour.

Chip4 alliance: A US-led coalition committed to ensuring the uninterrupted supply of chips (i.e. semiconductors or integrated circuits) around the world. The alliance consists of the US, Japan, South Korea, and Taiwan. The objective of this informal alliance, formed in 2023, was to prevent China from manipulating the global chip market.

Chips: Tiny pieces of semiconducting material like silicon. Used to generate AI and/or operate 'smart' devices like mobile phones, etc. Complex technical processes are needed to accomplish these objectives.

Civil AI (resolution, etc): The United Nations General Assembly (UNGA) has, for example, adopted resolutions on civil AI, which refers to the AI used in economic, educational and other non-military applications.

Cloud: A system that allows its users to store their data and/or access various computing services. In technical terms, 'cloud' consists of remote 'servers' that can be accessed through the 'internet' to store as well as manage and process data.

Computing power: This refers to the ability or capacity of a computer or a network of computers to process data and carry out complex calculations. A key factor in assessing the AI prowess of a state or an entity is its respective aggregate computing power.

Consensus: A general agreement among the stakeholders on any particular issue. On major international issues such as the reform of the United Nations Security Council, any proposal for consensus could mean the necessity of concurrence by every stakeholder.

Cyber sovereignty: The term means that all internet-related matters in the virtual environment (cyberspace) originating in or accessible to a state should come under its sovereignty (i.e. paramount authority) for regulatory purposes.

Cyberspace (Cyber domain, etc.): The term refers to a notional non-physical environment or a virtual environment in which real communications occur, often through the medium of computers.

Cyber warfare: Computer-aided attack, usually by a state or coalition of states, against its adversary's (or even adversaries') military assets. Successful virtual attack(s) in cyberspace will have a real impact, though. Computer-aided verbal attacks in cyberspace amount to a cyber war of words.

Data/datasets: A dataset is an organised list (or table) of statistics, often including basic facts relating to any particular subject. Datasets are used by the innovator (or developer) of an AI system (or model) to 'train' it to 'learn' and perform the intended task. In other words, datasets are used for 'machine learning' in the field of AI.

Deepfake: This term is used to describe false images that look like they are real. In the field of AI, such images are created by using machines (or devices) that 'learn' deeply from the relevant datasets and/or images.

Digital (technology, domain, etc.): As commonly understood, these terms refer to the science relating to the creation and use of computerised gadgets like the mobile phone and even systems such as the internet.

Digital authoritarianism: The politics of tightly controlling the development, deployment and use of digital technologies within the jurisdiction of a state or a group of like-minded states.

Digital democracy: The politics of allowing freedom to develop, deploy and use digital technologies within the borders of a state or a coalition of like-minded states.

Digital divide (also, digital gap): As commonly understood, the term refers to the difference between those with advanced skills in innovating or using digital technologies and those with little or no such skill. Such a difference (or divide or gap) exists within some states and between the states at different levels of scientific and technological progress.

Digital (also AI) protectionism: The term describes a state's policies aimed at guarding the 'secrets' of its own digital and AI technologies. High import tariffs are usually levied by the states practising trade protectionism. However, the digital and AI protectionism of a state means restricting or stopping its relevant exports to countries considered to be its competitors or adversaries.

Emotional intelligence: A person's capacity to understand one's own and other people's emotions at the same time. AI, while being simulated human intelligence but not a physical person, is not known to possess emotional intelligence. At least, not so far.

Escape velocity: The speed at which an object (for example, a spacecraft) escapes Earth's gravitational pull and enters Space. Metaphorically, for example, AI technology is developing so fast that it might escape from human control altogether.

Five Eyes: It is a five-nation alliance formed exclusively for the sharing of intelligence or information gathered through spying. The alliance comprises the United States, the United Kingdom, Canada, Australia and New Zealand.

Fractured reality: Reality with two or more aspects. Used in this monograph to denote the spheres of influence of competing states in a common geographical or technological space.

Frankenstein's monster: A fictional character's (Frankenstein's) destructive creation. In the realm of AI, the so-far-unrealised fear that an AI model or system might harm or ruin its human creator.

Freudian slip: An error, or more broadly, a statement, that reveals the subconscious feelings or intentions of the person concerned. In geopolitics, a statement meant to mislead or divert attention from reality without appearing to do so.

G7: Group of seven rich industrialised countries led by the US openly or in a subtle manner. Neither China, the world's second-largest economy, nor India, a gradually rising economy, is a member of this grouping.

G20: Group of 20 major economies – comprising both the developed countries and the emerging economies on the upward trajectory of development. China, which resembles a developed country in a few areas, and aspirational India are in the category of emerging economies.

GGE: Group of Governmental Experts (at the United Nations) dealing with one specialised area or another.

GPAI: Global Partnership on AI, an expanding international forum. India hosted a GPAI meeting in 2023.

GPU: Graphics Processing Unit. It is a chip with parallel processing capability. Used for graphics as well as AI.

Geopolitics (geopolitical): In practice on the world stage today, geopolitics is the targeted exercise of power by a state or a coalition of states against its real, potential, or presumed rival(s) or even towards its partner(s).

Geostrategy (also geostrategic): Strategy or well-considered plan based on the geopolitical considerations of the country or party concerned. Geostrategic affairs are often driven by the military or defence agenda of the country or party concerned.

Global governance: Governance is a continuous process of setting, implementing and updating policies to ensure perpetual stability and progress at the national, sub-national or international level. Governance at the national and sub-national levels is achieved by enacting and enforcing laws and rules, etc. Global governance is possible through bilateral or multilateral agreements among states and/or through agreements or resolutions in international organisations.

Globalism (also globalist): The targeted projection or exercise of power by a state or a coalition of states in world affairs of any kind. Also, deep interest in world affairs with or without an agenda or plan to project or exercise power on the international stage.

Global South: The term is used to identify the developing countries as a collective group, regardless of differences among the members in their respective levels of economic development.

Grey Zone (s): In international relations, grey zones concerning advanced technologies (as in this monograph) refer to the high-tech domains with inadequate governance norms or with no governance at all. (The term is amplified in Chapter 1).

Grey-zone activities: A state or a coalition's assertive and/or intimidatory actions against its real or presumed adversary (or adversaries) – without crossing the red line of waging war.

Heartbeat of Algorithm: The most essential feature of the algorithm that actually sustains it – like in the case of heartbeat for human life.

Hegemony (also hegemonic): In international relations, the real or presumed dominance by a state or a coalition over other countries. The term is generally used by the 'affected' side to decry the 'illegitimate' exercise of power by the domineering state or coalition.

High-tech bloc thinking: In the geopolitics of advanced technologies, the collective perceptions of a group of states. Such perceptions are orchestrated by the leader of that group or bloc of 'like-minded' countries.

High-tech candour: This is a term coined to describe a situation of frank views on advanced technologies.

High-tech core of the times: This is a term coined to describe the most essential (or core) technology among all the advanced technologies of any prevalent period of time. In this monograph, digital and cyberspace technologies are seen as constituting such a core in the age of AI.

Human-centric: This is a term used in the international statements on AI by mid-2024. The idea is that all aspects of AI must be kept under human control all the time.

Hyper-technology (also hyper-tech and high-tech): This is a simple term for the most advanced technology (hyper-technology) among all the higher technologies at any given time. Hyper-technology and high-tech are terms used interchangeably in this monograph because the rapidly advancing AI belongs to both categories.

iCET: Initiative on Critical and Emerging Technologies, a joint effort by the United States of America and India to cooperate in these domains. AI figures prominently in this initiative.

International law: This is a term that has come to mean different things to different countries. Generally, international law relating to any subject is a collection of norms and standards or rules that are applicable to all or some relevant states. Agreements among all or some relevant states (as the case might be) form the foundation of international law.

Internet freedom: This refers to the freedom of people to create and/or access online information in cyberspace. Some states, like China, view internet freedom as a violation of their respective national sovereign right to control or regulate online information.

Light years: Far from being a measure of time, 'light year' is a measure of distance in astronomy or the science relating to Outer Space. A 'light year' is the enormous distance that light covers at its phenomenal speed in the course of one year. In this monograph, the term 'light years' is used metaphorically to denote the strategic distance (or difference) between two states or two coalitions.

Maoist: This is a term derived from the name of the revolutionary leader Mao Zedong of the People's Republic of China. In mainstream national or international politics and diplomacy, a Maoist is a person inspired by Mao Zedong's authoritarian leadership and/or strategic thinking. In non-conventional terms, a Maoist is a political militant.

Mindscape: This author has conceptualised 'Mindscape' as a mental realm. This is like a 'landscape' in relation to physical land. Hyper-advanced technologies like those required to explore and utilise AI cyber-digital domains, for example, constitute the new mindscape in the 21st century.

Multilateralism (also multilateral): The term defines the process of negotiations among numerous states on any subject of their shared interest. Agreements reached through such a process are the products of multilateralism, as different from bilateral agreements between just two states.

NASDAQ: National Association of Securities Dealers Automated Quotations – a worldwide electronic marketplace.

NITI Aayog: National Institution for Transforming India (the updated and upgraded Planning Commission of India).

P5: Five Permanent Members of the United Nations Security Council – China, France, Russia, United Kingdom, United States of America. For the critics, 'P5' also stands for the Privileged Five because each of these five countries has the individual right to veto any decision by a majority in the UNSC.

Pacing challenge: A continuous challenge which keeps pace with the relevant state's continuous response.

Pentagon: United States of America's Department of Defence Headquarters.

Pyramid of Global AI Powers: A metaphorical way of describing a real or imaginary hierarchy of countries with proven prowess in AI. The term is derived from the structural appearance of the pyramids of ancient Egypt.

Quad: A forum of four 'like-minded' countries in the Indo-Pacific region to promote their shared security and strategic interests through dialogue and cooperation. The forum – comprises the US, Japan, India, and Australia. Quad is increasingly focused on high-tech issues, including those relating to AI.

Quantum computing: A highly complex computing system with the potential to exponentially increase the power of data processing for AI purposes.

Rules-based international order: Conceptualised by the US, the rules-based international order is, at best, a variant of international law. Critics see the rules-based order as a smokescreen for a selective interpretation of international law so as to promote the interests of the US-led West.

Semiconductor: As is implicit in the term itself, a semiconductor is a material, like silicon, with inherent electrical conductivity, which is not as strong as that of a good conductor. Very useful as AI hardware, semiconductor is not an insulator, either.

Single global internet (also, universal internet): The worldwide web as a global public good with no national restrictions or bans on accessing it.

Sovereignty: The paramount enforceable authority of a state over the territories it administers legally under international law. An altogether different matter is the notional sovereignty of a state over the territories it legally claims without actually controlling them.

Speed of thought: A colourful way of describing the apparent speed at which an advancement in AI materialises as soon as the innovator thinks about it.

State-of-the-art (technology, etc.): As commonly understood, it is the latest advancement in any technological domain.

Techplomacy: A portmanteau of technology and diplomacy. Diplomacy powered by the technological prowess of a state or group of states.

Techno-autocracy: Authoritarian control by a state over all matters relating to technologies, usually within its national jurisdiction. In international relations, the advocacy of autocratic controls over the inter-state flow of technologies. Actions by state(s) to enforce such controls are also a feature of this kind of diplomacy.

Techno-democracy: Democratic freedoms allowed by a state for technological advancements, usually within its sovereign jurisdiction. In international relations, the advocacy of the free flow of technologies across national boundaries. Furthermore, the term applies to the actions by state(s) to ensure such a free flow of technologies.

UNGA: United Nations General Assembly, where all member-states of the UN are represented.

UNSC: United Nations Security Council, widely regarded as the world's apex forum for the strategic military affairs of all states. Broadly defined, the Council's mandate is to address all issues concerning peace and security across the world. The compact Council has 15 members – the P5 and 10 non-permanent members elected periodically through a rotational system. Much international focus now is on the issue of reforming the UNSC to make it truly representative of the UN member-states. A novel idea of an "AI solution" for UNSC reform is explored in this monograph.

Unilateralism (unilateral): As opposed to multilateralism, the term 'unilateralism' applies to the effort(s) of a state or coalition or alliance to address the international issue(s) by its own free will – without consulting or cooperating with the other stakeholders.

US characteristics: In some contrast to 'Chinese characteristics', the term applies to America's unique capabilities and achievements in almost all fields of human endeavour.

1

An Emerging Era of a New Mindscape of Grey Zones

The critical, emerging, and elusive domains of highly advanced science and technology of the 21st century can be harnessed beneficially in the global commons. Practical norms for the governance of hyper-advanced tech domains are required for such a happy state of affairs. However, in the first quarter of this century, such norms were neither fully in place nor easily enforceable, even if they had already been adopted in multilateral settings. Such a crucial aspect of little or no global governance in the domains of hyper-advanced technology characterises them as 'grey zones'. Accessible to states, non-state actors, including armed groups, and the general population, two indispensable grey zones are (1) artificial intelligence (AI) as well as (2) the inter-related cyber and digital domains.

AI and cyber-digital capabilities are being increasingly deployed for both civil and military applications by state actors and, in some cases, by non-state players as well. Furthermore, AI and the cyber-digital domains complement each other. Separately, numerous are the United Nations General Assembly (UNGA) resolutions on the exploration of outer space. However, the space-faring powers are more conscious of the utility of outer space for their respective national interest rather than the global good.

A significant reason for my perception of the hyper-advanced tech domains as grey zones is their inherent attributes. The relevant technologies produce targeted benefits and/or cause harm when deployed by states and non-state actors to pursue their own objectives, legitimate or otherwise.

These grey zones at the new expanding frontiers of knowledge in the 21st century form a mindscape, meaning that the relevant foundational know-how is the human mind's imaginative creation. AI and the cyber-digital domains are certainly real (not false) in their impact. But they are essentially non-tangible systems except for the material, such as, for example, computer hardware, used to deploy or access them.

In striking difference, outer space is very much a visible domain, although ordinary people may see it as a vacuous area. Significant, however, is the know-how required to access outer space and put it to economic and military purposes, which is the imaginative creation of the human mind. Viewed from this perspective, outer space, too, is a feature of the mindscape.

Grey zones of hyper-advanced technology are different from the grey-zone activities of some states. For example, the People's Republic of China's (PRC's) military moves along and across the disputed Sino-Indian boundary since mid-2020 are seen in Delhi as grey-zone activities. Typically, such activities are coercive policies and actions pursued by any state against its actual or perceived or potential rival(s) without crossing the red line of war. These policies and actions are, therefore, unregulated under the laws of war.

Future wars could be launched from any domain – conventional, nuclear or a grey zone of hyper-advanced technology such as AI, cyber-digital space or outer space. Thus it can be argued that Geopolitics drives grey-zone activities. It also shapes the challenges of governance in the grey zones of hyper-advanced technology.

Apt indeed is the hyphenated adjective of 'grey-zone' for the often-surreptitious activities of some states like China below the red line of war against their perceived adversaries like India. In contrast, the non-hyphenated 'grey zones' refer to the hyper-advanced domains of science and technology where governance has become a worldwide concern. This grammatical distinction may well define the grammar of geopolitics in this emerging age of AI.

The grey-zone tactics are driven by geopolitics. Imaginative innovations in science and technology, almost at the speed of light, propel developments in the grey zones like AI, the cyber-digital realm, etc. A commonality is that geopolitics induces grey-zone tactics while – separately – complicating the governance of grey zones of hyper-advanced technology.

Geopolitics itself is often viewed differently by different countries and scholars at different times as well. In the late 19th century and early 20th century, Alfred Mahan and Halford Mackinder had respectively conceptualised sea power and command over geography as the geopolitics of a state.[1] According to India's former National Security Advisor and former Foreign Secretary Shivshankar Menon, "in popular parlance, geopolitics is almost synonymous with power politics". In his view, the "long-term drivers of a state's quest for power" are "geography, history, economics and demography".[2] Thus it can be argued that Geopolitics today is the targeted exercise of power by a state or a coalition of states against its real or potential rival(s) or even partner(s).

Governance at High-Tech Pinnacle

Broadly, the aim of governance is to ensure the stability and progress of state(s) or group(s) of states in any legitimate sector of human endeavour. The same norm applies to any state's control of the activities of non-state actors, including non-state armed groups.

Governance is a continuous process of setting, implementing, and updating policies. This is done through laws and rules to sustain stability and orderliness at the national, sub-national or international level, as the case might be.

For example, the hallmark of good governance in a state is its progress with stability in all aspects of human endeavour – ranging from citizens' welfare to foreign policy. Bad governance is exemplified by the disruption or destruction of activities deemed to be legitimate at the group, national, or international level. Grey zones at the fast-expanding pinnacle of science and technology, therefore, require good governance at the national, sub-national and international levels.

There has been a growing global alarm over the disturbing and disruptive impact of some dramatic developments in the deployment of AI in particular. 'Deepfakes', with a self-explanatory meaning, fall under this dim light. Non-state actors seem to have been the first movers in creating AI's disconcerting impact. Not ruled out, though, is the potentially destabilising geopolitical behaviour of some states like China and the United States of America in deploying AI for hegemonic military purposes.

As an emerging hyper-advanced technology, AI is embedded in China's strategic capabilities and military doctrine. The name of the military game in China is "the development and utilisation of new types of combat forces".[3]

Foremost among these new types are AI-enabled combat forces, i.e. weapon systems.

The US has styled itself as "a global leader in the responsible development and use of weapon systems with autonomous functions", notably AI-enabled arms. Explaining a US directive in this regard in 2023, a Pentagon official emphasised that "AI is likely to play an increasing role in a range of systems and capabilities".[4]

India's quest for AI-powered national defence was articulated by Prime Minister Narendra Modi in July 2022 on the occasion of launching a book, 'AI Def: Artificial Intelligence in Defence'. In a message, he said, "It is crucial to promote customisation and uniqueness of our defence systems for a strategic edge over the adversaries (emphasis added)".[5] Nonetheless, India "has no intention to rule the world", Defence Minister Rajnath Singh noted but emphasised the need to develop the country's AI arms capabilities. The objective was that "no country can even think of ruling [over] us", he said.[6] This is as good a signal as any that India wants to reinforce its nuclear-armed deterrence with AI-arms deterrence.

Globally, it is likely that AI, cyber-digital know-how and outer space will be increasingly deployed for national or multilateral military purposes in conflict situations. The United Nations Security Council (UNSC) may, therefore, have to set norms for the governance of these areas of humanity's mindscape. But the Council is not well-positioned, at this writing, for this truly challenging task. (This caveat is explained in Chapter 7 of this book.)

Eight decades after World War II and the creation of the UN a gradual reform of the functions of the UNSC is urgently needed. For optimal global governance of the grey zones of advanced technologies, the UNSC must be fully reconstituted to reflect the geostrategic mosaic of the 21st century. Otherwise, even 'binding' decisions by the non-reformed UNSC – on AI or cyber-digital security – may remain on paper. These might include any relevant decisions after the UN Summit of the Future scheduled for September 2024.

Already, the US has begun to be sceptical of a basic norm that all UNSC resolutions are always 'binding' on all UN member states. This principle is enshrined in the UN Charter. However, on March 25, 2024, the US sidelined this principle after abstaining from voting on a binding UNSC resolution on Israel-Hamas ceasefire in Gaza. Explaining the abstention, US Permanent Representative to the UN, Linda Thomas-Greenfield, characterised the resolution, which was duly adopted, as "nonbinding" on her country.[7] The relevant reasoning is linked to Washington's status in the UNSC. Ostensibly, for historical reasons, the US is one of the five permanent members (P5) of the UNSC, while the others are China, France, Russia, and the United Kingdom. Until this is written, each P5 member remains empowered to veto any UNSC resolution at any time.

While speaking after the Council adopted the Gaza ceasefire resolution on March 24, 2024, Linda Thomas-Greenfield did not say why a UNSC resolution could be 'nonbinding' on the UN member-state(s). But the US seems to have had a reason. Hence, it can be argued that the US had begun to explore a creative 'caveat' that a P5 member's abstention from voting on any UNSC resolution could render it nonbinding on that country.

The possible insightful reasoning for such an action is that having refrained from voting for or against a UNSC resolution, a P5 member, with the vetoing power, need not necessarily abide by the substantive matter at stake. Abstention signifies practical disapproval of the overall substance of a resolution, which, in effect, becomes nonbinding on the P5 member concerned. In this nuanced reasoning, a P5 member's non-exercise of veto on any UNSC resolution does not amount to any kind of conditional approval of the substantive matter(s) at stake. By refraining from vetoing, the P5 member merely steps aside to let the other members decide. The same reasoning applies to a P5 member's refusal to cast a positive vote. Viewed in this subtle perspective, the abstention(s) by P5 member(s) would give each or all the bandwidth of agnosticism towards the substance of the relevant resolution(s). In all, this episode marks potential 'creativity' about 'nonbinding' UNSC resolutions! However, it should be noted that this reasoning has not been stated by the US. Nevertheless, this precedent could well influence the future course of UNSC's activism on the enormous military implications of AI for life and work.

A few noteworthy steps regarding AI were taken by the UN system before the flutter over the potential status of UNSC resolutions on substantive matters. In October 2023, the governance of AI was firmly placed as a key topic for the UN Summit of the Future in September 2024.[8]

In December 2023, the UNGA adopted a nonbinding AI arms (weapons) resolution. Following up in March 2024, the UNGA adopted a civil AI resolution – also a nonbinding document. Under the UN Charter, all UNGA resolutions are non-binding in their impact. Nonetheless, they reflect international public opinion, as articulated by member-states in the chamber. Not many states can nonchalantly defy such an opinion.

The steps taken at the UN with regard to AI, therefore, produced a cumulative sense of calibrated momentum towards the global governance of this key grey zone. No less important, the UN Summit of the Future was tasked, from the beginning, to unveil a 'Global Digital Compact' through final negotiations by political leaders of states. (These developments are evaluated in later chapters of this book).

Scope of This Book

The ambient focus in this book is geopolitics. Issues and solutions for the international governance of two highly advanced grey zones are explored. This is done extensively in the context of the progressing state of affairs in AI. The reason for this choice is that AI is increasingly becoming the strategic flavour of our times in both civil and military domains. In far lesser but relevant detail, the governance of the cyber-digital domain is also explored. Inevitably and intentionally, this choice promotes brevity in a monograph.

China's grey-zone activities against India, briefly noted above, constitute an important aspect of Asian and global geopolitics in the first quarter of the 21st century. Beijing's attempts at coercion in military and other matters, like, for example, the refusal of visas for Indian citizens from some parts of the country, have raised concerns in Delhi. At this writing, Chinese President Xi Jinping has also not followed up on his invitation to Modi in 2019 for their next (i.e. third) 'informal' and candid conversation.

Besides India, some Southeast Asian countries and Japan have also often felt the negative impact of Chinese grey-zone activities. Beijing does not fully disclose its strategy in pursuing these operations, therefore colouring them with the imagery of greyness. Not fully concealed, though, by China is its intention of trying to intimidate India, for example, below the red line of actual war. This aspect also brings China's grey-zone activities into sharp focus.

Ashok Kantha, formerly India's External Affairs Secretary (East) and Ambassador to China, told this author[9] as follows: "China's high-level troop deployments and intrusions across the Sino-Indian Line of Actual Control since 2020 have created a 'new normal' in the bilateral engagement, according to Chinese officials and scholars". He said "they expect us [Indians] to accept this [new normal] as the basis for continuing the [Sino-Indian] engagement process".

Unilateral imposition of sanctions by the US on other countries, including India occasionally, is also a grey-zone phenomenon. Being outside the UN's purview, these US sanctions, too, are coloured by the imagery of the greyness of diplomacy. In recent times, the US and China have traded reciprocal sanctions as well.

America imposes sanctions without the UN's approval but within a bandwidth between a hegemonic but sovereign exercise of power and legitimacy under international law. Both the US and China cite their respective national interest in this regard. But their actions have acquired the diplomatic complexion of greyness. Mainly because these two countries neither fully disclose nor fully conceal their respective strategic interests in resorting to grey-zone tactics.

This book is focused on the geopolitical diplomacy of administering AI – a major grey zone at the high end of science and technology in the first quarter of the 21st century.

However, the geopolitics of China's grey-zone activities, especially towards India, as briefly noted, have not been explored. The main reason for this omission is that both India and China are very possessive about bilateralism in their engagement with each other. Surely, this is a hallmark of their respective strategic culture as major powers. From this perspective, there is no scope or need for any kind of global governance or management of the Sino-Indian bilateral engagements. Considerations of brevity, too, in a monograph do not necessitate a detailed discussion of China's grey-zone tactics against India.

For brevity and clarity in this book, the governance of just AI is explored expansively. In far lesser detail, the cyber-digital realm, which provides the platform for AI, is briefly considered in one chapter. These two grey zones straddle the expanding pinnacle of science and technology.

The scientific and technological foundations of grey zones are beyond the scope of this book on geopolitics. Although some regional and functional groups focus on AI and the cyber-digital domain, the UN is the prime theatre for the governance of the grey zones of hyper-advanced technology. There is, therefore, a wide-angled focus in this book on the UN's role in regulating the development and deployment of AI, the high-tech flavour of our times.

Notes

1. The early ideas of geopolitics are often attributed to Alfred Thayer Mahan, *The Influence of Sea Power upon History1660–1783* (published in 1890), and Halford Mackinder, *The Geographical Pivot of History* (theorised in 1904).
2. Shivshankar Menon, *India and Asian Geopolitics: The Past, Present* (India: Penguin Random House India, 2021), p. 4.
3. Xinhua, "Xi Focus: Xi stresses deepening reform to comprehensively enhance strategic capabilities in emerging areas", *Xinhua*, https://english.news.cn/20240307/2b19b93e1002413091745e3ab8a94de3/c.html (Last accessed on April 23, 2024). See also *South China Morning Post*, "China's Xi Jinping issues hi-tech military call in push for integrated armed forces", *South China Morning Post*, https://www.scmp.com/news/china/military/article/3254735/chinas-xi-jinping-issues-hi-tech-military-call-push-integrated-armed-forces (Last accessed on April 25, 2024).
4. US Department of Defence, "DOD Updates Autonomy in Weapons System Directive", *U.S. Department of Defense, Defense Department News*, https://www.defense.gov/News/News-Stories/Article/Article/3278065/dod-updates-autonomy-in-weapons-system-directive/ (Last accessed on April 25, 2024).
5. "AI Def: Artificial Intelligence in Defence", *Department of Defence Production*, Ministry of Defence, Government of India, https://www.ddpmod.gov.in/sites/default/files/ai.pdf.
6. "Raksha Mantri launches 75 Artificial Intelligence products/technologies during first-ever 'AI in Defence' symposium & exhibition in New Delhi; Terms AI as a revolutionary step in the development of humanity", *Ministry of Defence*, PIB, https://pib.gov.in/PressReleasePage.aspx?PRID=1840740.
7. US Mission to the UN, "Explanation of Vote Delivered by Ambassador Linda Thomas-Greenfield Following the Adoption of a UNSC Resolution on the Situation in the Middle East", United States Mission to the United Nations, https://usun.usmission.gov/explanation-of-vote-delivered-by-ambassador-linda-thomas-greenfield-following-the-adoption-of-a-unsc-resolution-on-the-situation-in-the-middle-east/.
8. António Guterres, "Secretary-General's remarks at press conference launching High-Level Advisory Body on Artificial Intelligence", *United Nations*, https://www.un.org/sg/en/content/sg/speeches/2023-10-26/secretary-general%E2%80%99s-remarks-press-conference-launching-high-level-advisory-body-artificial-intelligence%C2%A0.
9. This author's telephone conversation with Ambassador Ashok Kantha on March 10, 2024.

2

Artificial Intelligence: Technology Unbound

It is universally understood that the computer-science-based simulation of human intelligence is artificial intelligence (AI). Far exceeding the original expectations of many, it has now become a potential architect of the future of life and work for humanity. As a result, the global governance of AI has become a core interest of humanity.

Abraham Lincoln, the iconic former President of the United States (US), is credited with this tip for proactive action: The best way to predict the future is to create it. Defying this tip, though, innovators have created an amazing new technology known as AI, but they have been unable to predict its future. In varying degrees, such a curious lack of predictability has certainly shadowed many inventions over the millennia. The best previous example is the nuclear weapon, the ultimate future of which is still undetermined. However, AI, with its unpredictable future, seems to surpass all the previous products of science and technology – in terms of an eerie possibility of escaping human control absolutely.

A more serious concern, transcending such a possibility, is "the potential peril... whether AI might really destroy the human species, or even replace it". An international news magazine has posed a stark question in this regard – "Do we face an existential threat?"[1] An exploration of this question by three AI pioneers straddles both the catastrophic and optimistic scenarios.

In such a worldwide buzz, what indeed is AI? It is no longer a mere smart tool in the hands of its developers and intermediate- or end-users. An 'AI system' definition has been compiled and updated by the Organization for Economic Cooperation and Development (OECD) through consultations among its members.[2]

The long-winded but seemingly all-encompassing definition is as follows: "An AI system is a machine-based system that, for explicit or implicit objectives, infers, from the input it receives, how to generate outputs such as predictions, content, recommendations, or decisions that can influence physical or virtual environments. Different AI systems vary in their levels of autonomy and adaptiveness after deployment".[3] This wide-spectrum official definition contains conventional computer science jargons. However, the OECD's explanations of the terms clarify the meaning of AI in a manner that could help in understanding the geopolitics of this grey zone. As annotated by this author, the OECD points out the following distinctions. Any AI system's explicit objectives are those programmed for it by its human developer in a state or a territory without statehood. The implicit objectives are those that any AI system would either pursue as intended by its human developer or learn to pursue based on the developer's software.[4]

A human developer could be either a state's official or state-controlled actor or even a non-state activist anywhere in the world. 'Content' refers to the text produced by the so-called generative AI systems. Their decisions, recommendations or predictions – produced as output for the developers and intermediate- or end-users – constitute 'content'.

Important, as well, is the dual classification of 'physical' or 'virtual' environments. Logically, both these environments are said to be real in their respective avatar. Human beings easily recognise the difference between physical and virtual objects and/or situations. The autonomy of any AI system is its ability to act independently of the human developer's software design. This ability may be programmed in the software itself. Alternatively, the AI system could learn to become autonomous while it functions. Adaptiveness is said to be the AI system's ability to respond to the preferences of the intermediate- or end-users. Any AI system could become adaptive, regardless of whether these preferences have been programmed in the developer's software design.[5]

It is evident from this complexity that artificial intelligence is an unbound human-engineered domain. Its frontiers are expanding at almost the speed of thought. The adaptiveness of AI systems and, potentially, their expanding autonomous power may determine the future of life and work on Earth. There are plenty of concerns about AI-enabled deepfakes in the civilian sector. Serious opinions are also in vogue about the potential deployment of AI-powered autonomous weapons in the military domains.

Some deepfake images in the civilian sectors have already produced a chilling sense of unreality. Celebrities in different fields of legitimate human endeavour have been targeted through deepfakes. For decency and the personal privacy of those targeted, explicit references to deepfake images are avoided in this book.

AI for Good and Bad Use

A public statement by the United Nations Secretary-General Antonio Guterres merits serious attention. Launching a 'High-Level Multistakeholder Advisory Body on Artificial Intelligence' (hereinafter, UN's AI Advisory Body) in New York on October 26 2023, Guterres said, "The [world] has seen an extraordinary advance in the capabilities and use of artificial intelligence, through chatbots, voice cloning, image generators, video apps and more. Thanks to one such app, I had the surreal experience of watching myself deliver a speech in flawless Chinese – despite the fact that I do not speak Chinese, and the lips movement corresponded exactly to what I was saying. This is just one example of the incredible possibilities – and the potential dangers of AI."[6] Concerns cited by him as consequences of the AI abuse were (1) misinformation and disinformation about vital facts; (2) aggravation of the existing bias and the creation of new bias in social habits, besides greater discrimination in public life; (3) invasion of personal privacy, and surveillance of people by states and non-state actors; and (4) facilitation of fraud and human rights violations, among other malicious deeds which could spark a slide towards doomsday scenarios. On the positive side of the ledger, though, Guterres outlined the "transformative potential of AI for good."[7] As good examples of the AI-enabled possibilities, he cited (1) direct delivery of public services to the people in need – by "leapfrogging outdated technologies"; (2) efficient rollout of public health and education services; and (3) efforts to "supercharge climate action", among other social benefits.

India's Digital Public Infrastructure (DPI) is projected as a globally replicable example of direct delivery of public services.[8] Designed to ensure near-universal access to economic and health facilities in the most populous country, the DPI is powered by cyber and AI technologies. It is also recognised that the DPI has leapfrogged, or overflown, the old ineffective procedures in the direct delivery of public services. As a result, India is willing to share its DPI experiences with the Global South of developing countries.

India's 'Democratisation of Technology'

Prime Minister Narendra Modi showcased the Unified Payments Interface (UPI), widely regarded as a star of India's DPI, in an interview with Newsweek, a US magazine, in April 2024. In simple terms, UPI is a system that facilitates real-time payments through the use of mobile phones. PM Modi said, "UPI is a fine example of Indian innovation at its best. I see UPI as a simple tool that broke countless barriers, from financial barriers to geographical barriers. It has opened the world of digital transactions to the person at the last mile".[9] Hailing this as "democratisation of technology", Modi added that, "people should be trusted to adapt quickly to technology". Another "lesson" from the "success" of UPI, he emphasised, was that the technology should be "open, interoperable, scalable and secure".[10]

In the big picture, though, the uneven global distribution of AI power minimises the benefits it delivers and magnifies the concerns it causes. Alluding to this grim reality, Guterres noted: "AI expertise is concentrated in a handful of companies and countries. This could deepen global inequalities and turn digital divides into chasms". He was referring to the existing inequalities in accessing advanced communications technologies. Furthermore, he implicitly noted social and economic disparities within and between countries.

To mitigate such concerns and enhance the benefits, Guterres emphasised that the AI know-how must be "harnessed responsibly, and made accessible to all".[11] The AI-savvy countries were, in essence, asked to share their expertise with the developing countries, collectively known as the Global South. For a start, professional and social responsibility in designing and developing AI systems would safeguard 'social cohesion' in innovative countries. In such a milieu, the AI architects and their products could gain international trust. These were some of the open and subtle messages from Guterres.

Humanity's Manifest New Technology[12]

By the beginning of 2024, the UN identified AI as a new technology unbound (without actually using this term). This was evident from the previously unknown pace at which this technology was being unleashed (i.e. unbound). This was evident, too, from the sense of urgency shown by the UN's AI Advisory Body in its Interim Report on 'Governing AI for Humanity'. The Interim Report was meant to set the terms for the final report in time for the September 2024 UN Summit of the Future.

The Interim Report, launched on December 21, 2023, called for "grounding artificial intelligence in universal principles".[13] The core principles of international law were considered indispensable. A key objective was to prevent this amazing technology from attaining escape velocity and going out of human control. Tasks were also set for a 'potential institution' that could govern AI – by monitoring those states and non-state actors engaged in developing and deploying this technology.

Spawned by computer science, AI has actually been a manifest technology for decades. A member of the Indian Diaspora has played a significant role in the global development of AI. In 1994, Raj Reddy, an American citizen of Indian origin, won the highest global award in computer science for his contributions as a 'pioneer' in artificial intelligence and robotics. He was the first ethnic Asian (not just ethnic Indian) to have been recognised as one of the early AI pioneers.[14] He fostered a computer science institution at Carnegie Mellon University in the US and founded another in Hyderabad (India). He was also a co-chairman of a panel that advised the US President on information technology.

The chip industry of integrated circuits (or semiconductors) has made dramatic progress since AI was pioneered by several scientists. Chips like the Graphics Processing Units (GPUs) have, in particular, propelled AI to dizzying heights.[15] High-resolution surveillance devices and powerful kinetic weapons, both powered by AI, are two examples of this ongoing technological revolution.

Key sources of AI's phenomenal power are a diverse range of computer science software programmes known as 'algorithms'. The intermediate- and end-products of a physical or virtual kind, created by these complex algorithms, have either beneficial or harmful effects on the targeted object(s) or people. In simple terms, an algorithm is a software programme, often designed with sequential commands, for computer(s) or robot(s) to produce outcomes as desired by the developer(s). The algorithms designed so far, as of this writing, have certainly remained under human control without attaining autonomy that could produce serious scientific or geopolitical concerns.

AI is What AI Does

Indeed, the AI systems in vogue until this is written are believed to lag behind human intelligence in key aspects like real comprehension, deep reasoning, emotional intelligence, and consciousness. Nonetheless, AI models are known to study massive data at lightning speed, learn, draw conclusions, think, and provide answers relevant to the intermediate and/ or end-users of these systems. A very smart AI model could also become totally or functionally autonomous on its own manoeuvre or on the basis of the relevant software design itself. Even as 'benign' AI systems have proliferated, some designers of algorithms are suspected to have developed 'malign' AI models. Playful and/or harmful deepfakes fall into this latter category. It has also been difficult to trace the identities of algorithm designers except those seeking patents. Despite the deepfakes, as at the beginning of 2024, the fear that Frankenstein's monsters could emerge in the AI domain did not come true. Serious, though, is the UN's effort to prevent a grim scenario of the AI systems being able to undermine, if not overwhelm, human control over life and work.

A silver lining is that the international community is already sensitised to the potential risks inherent in the rapid strides being made by the ubiquitous algorithm designers. Nonetheless, it is an open question if the international community could address the potential risks by developing a worldwide system of issuing patents for algorithm designs.

In theory, algorithms are not easily patentable because these are essentially software programmes based on abstract ideas.[16] However, the physical products, developed on the basis of abstract algorithms, could be patented. China is said to hold the largest number of AI patents (not necessarily algorithm patents as such), being just ahead of the US and Japan.[17] The AI patents in these three front-running countries relate mainly to sub-disciplines like speech or image recognition, machine learning and robotics.[18] For China, the challenges of AI are in algorithm research, the indigenous development of software, and the inadequate technical maturity of the relevant chips.[19]

Patents for algorithms or, more precisely, for AI systems might, in theory, enhance their trustworthiness. This is true of the civilian sectors. However, for national militaries, though, the functional efficacy of their weapon systems powered by AI is often more important than patents. In the public domain, including at the UN, AI-powered Lethal Autonomous Weapons (LAWS) are considered to reflect the most dangerous application of this advanced futurist technology.

Weaponisation of AI and Ethics

During the UN Security Council's first-ever debate on AI, on July 18 2023, Guterres called for the "prohibition of [those] lethal autonomous weapons [which are deployable] without human control".[20] LAWS, also known as 'killer robots', reveal the extent of technological advancement in the military use of AI.

A UN expert consultant on AI ethics and governance, Cansu Canca, also a philosopher, traces the AI-prowess of LAWS as follows: "Killer robots, or lethal autonomous weapons as they are called, include all systems that have capacity to kill and that engage with the target without human intervention, following the initial programming instructions. They can detect, identify, and attack their targets. LAWS are distinct from other fully or partially remotely-operated military systems because they [the killer robots] fully eliminate the need for a human officer's approval or control to complete their tasks".[21]

Amplifying the crucial ethical aspects of the use of LAWS, she raises the following questions: "Can LAWS distinguish combatants from civilians, and can they reliably judge the context [of war]? Can they decide and act in a way that values human life? And if they operate on complex machine learning [AI] models, who is accountable for their errors? Do they create a responsibility gap in military operations?"[22] These ethical issues in the military usage of AI-powered LAWS call for clear answers as the advancement of AI is happening at the speed of light.

Pentagon's Five AI-Ethical Principles

To "lead in AI ethics and the lawful use of AI systems", the US Defence Department (Pentagon) adopted a set of principles on February 24 2020. Three main objectives were cited for the accelerated adoption of AI ethics by the US together with its allies and partners who were not identified, though. India was, and continues to be, a US partner. According to Defence

Secretary Mark Esper, under Trump's administration, the objectives were to "maintain [America's] strategic position, prevail on [the] future battlefields, and safeguard the rules-based international order".[23]

The first two objectives continue to reflect an enduring US aspiration which was, and arguably still is, condemned by China as the unalloyed hegemony of a bully.[24] Nonetheless, in Washington's view, the 'future battlefields' could be theatres of weaponised artificial intelligence. Furthermore, the correlation between America's preference for 'the rules-based international order' (not international law) and the weaponisation of AI is a geopolitical novelty.

What are the Pentagon's ethical safeguards against the potential abuse of the weaponisation of AI? The safeguards or principles were classified under five areas of guidelines for the good behaviour of American military personnel, both combatants and non-combatants alike. On a note of assurance, the Pentagon outlined "responsible, equitable, traceable, reliable and governable" categories of good conduct that the US military personnel would observe.[25] Being "responsible for the development, deployment and use of AI capabilities" for warfare, the relevant US personnel "will exercise appropriate levels of judgment and care", the Pentagon asserted.[26] The need for responsible behaviour of personnel was reinforced by the fact that the weaponisation of AI capabilities was a new technological revolution in military affairs.

With the AI revolution in military applications continuing, at this writing, the US and its ally, Israel, are generally perceived to be ahead of the curve. Going forward, it might be useful to have independent assessments of the US military personnel's observance of all the AI-related norms of behaviour.

As for the norm of equitable conduct, the Pentagon pledged to "take deliberate steps to minimise the unintended bias in AI capabilities". This could mean that human control over the AI prowess of LAWS would be maintained in conflict situations as well. To be noted, however, is the significance of the pledge to 'minimise' rather than eliminate "the unintended bias in AI capabilities". This could mean that the Pentagon kept for itself the option of matching any adversarial state which might use LAWS without human control in conflict situations. As already noted, LAWS without human control, especially those with the AI signature, could lead to indiscriminate killings, a matter of deep concern to the UN.

Pentagon's 'traceable' guideline was spelt out as follows: "AI capabilities will be developed and deployed such that relevant personnel possess an appropriate understanding of the technology, development processes, and operational methods applicable to AI capabilities". Clearly, the objective in formulating this norm was to try and ensure that anything going wrong could be traced to the relevant personnel and functional level.

To ensure reliable and well-defined [military] uses of AI capabilities, the Pentagon pledged to test their safety, security and effectiveness throughout their entire life cycles. These four norms were conceptualised mainly to ensure responsible personnel and reliable AI capabilities for war preparation.

Overarching these norms was the Pentagon's pledge to remain responsible in any actual conflict situation as well. Under the governable guideline, the Pentagon sought two objectives – ensure the functioning of AI-powered war machines and address any malfunction. For the first objective, the designing and engineering of AI capabilities would have "the ability to detect and avoid unintended consequences" while retaining the ability to perform as intended.

As a responsible and trustworthy AI power, the US would make sure that its AI war machine could "disengage or deactivate deployed systems that demonstrate unintended behaviour".[27] This kind of assurance was meant to reinforce US credentials for a leading role in any form of global governance of the grey zone of AI.

How 'Artificial' is Intelligence?

AI sceptics, if any, might harbour a couple of misperceptions. The science and art of AI (different from the gadgets it helps to create) belong to the virtual world of computers and cyberspace. Some might, therefore, mistake the artificiality of AI for unreality. Evident, though, is the fact that the artificiality of AI is just as real as the impact of cyberspace, for example. In another misperception, the intelligence aspect of AI might be mistaken for spying, instead of abstract thinking, the mental or neural springboard for AI.

Real or apocryphal, the story of Stanislav Petrov illustrates the fine line between artificiality as a virtual reality and intelligence as a mental or neural phenomenon. Petrov is said to have violated the Soviet Union's protocol for retaliation against the US on September 26, 1983, but prevented a potential nuclear clash between the two superpowers.[28] Working at an early-warning base outside Moscow, Petrov 'dismissed' as 'false alarm'[29] five signals from an artificial Soviet satellite that indicated America's launch of nuclear-armed missiles against his country. As a well-trained lieutenant colonel, if he had reported the satellite message to the relevant Soviet authorities, Moscow might have launched an actual nuclear missile strike against the US. In that event, Washington could have engaged the Soviets in an exchange of catastrophic nuclear weapons fire. Such was the intended substance of this narrative in 2013 about an unusual Cold-War episode 30 years earlier.

Similar versions of this episode gained much publicity after Petrov, said to have belonged to the Soviet Air Defence Forces, was reported to have died in 2017. One version said, "It was later determined [i.e. after the episode in 1983] that Russian [meaning Soviet] satellites must have mistaken sunlight reflecting off clouds for [American] nuclear missiles".[30] If true, it is indeed an astonishing mistake by an 'intelligent' spy satellite! In another version, Petrov "reasoned that if the United States really were to start a nuclear war, it would do so with more than five missiles".[31]

In all, though, a knowledgeable Kremlinologist familiar with the Soviet-American Cold War tensions does not confirm this episode. Furthermore, the West often plays up the Soviet/Russian 'failures', while officials in Moscow, both during and after the Cold War, would have preferred golden silence over such an alleged episode.

Even if apocryphal, therefore, the story of Stanislav Petrov's human intelligence prevailing over an artificial satellite's 'false alarm' seems relevant to assessing the unparalleled AI power. Referring to this reported Soviet 'episode', a young Indian computer engineer, Vijay Lakshminarayanan, at a NASDAQ-listed corporation, emphasised the utmost importance of "harmonising AI with human ingenuity".[32]

While human ingenuity will remain essential for harnessing AI for global good, this hyper-advanced technology is widely believed to be on a [metaphoric] quantum-leap trajectory. Ramakanth Desai, an Indian electronics and communications engineer conversant with the dynamics of AI, agrees in scientific terms as well. His view: "The evolution of quantum computing (QC) will make a huge difference, enabling AI technologies to realise their full potential. QC will accelerate algorithms, solve optimisation problems faster, and perform complex simulations. Quantum-enhanced AI algorithms promise more efficient and powerful AI systems".[33]

Notes

1. TIME Special Edition, *Artificial Intelligence: A New Age of Possibilities*, 2024 (pdf), pp. 24 – 27.
2. China and India, both major powers, are not members (being only "Key Partners") of the US-driven Organization for Economic Cooperation and Development (OECD).
3. Stuart Russell, Karine Perset, Marko Grobelnik, "Updates to the OECD's definition of an AI system explained", *OECD*, https://oecd.ai/en/wonk/ai-system-definition-update.
4. Ibid. (definitions, as annotated by this author).
5. Ibid.
6. António Guterres, "Secretary-General's remarks at press conference launching High-Level Advisory Body on Artificial Intelligence", *United Nations*, https://www.un.org/sg/en/content/sg/speeches/2023-10-26/secretary-general%E2%80%99s-remarks-press-conference-launching-high-level-advisory-body-artificial-intelligence%C2%A0.
7. Ibid.
8. "PM addresses G20 Digital Economy Ministers' Meet", *Prime Minister's Office*, PIB, https://pib.gov.in/PressReleasePage.aspx?PRID=1950321.
9. Dev Pragad, Nancy Cooper, Danish Manzoor Bhat, "Exclusive Interview: Narendra Modi and the Unstoppable Rise of India", *Newsweek Magazine*, https://www.newsweek.com/2024/04/19/exclusive-interview-narendra-modi-unstoppable-rise-india-1888678.html.
10. Ibid.
11. Guterres, n.6.
12. The term "manifest" is used in the sense of an evident and profound reality, as for example in the term "manifest destiny". AI is widely perceived as an evident and profound technology of the future (beginning now).
13. "UN AI Advisory Body calls for grounding artificial intelligence in universal principles, suggests tasks for a potential institution on AI governance", *United Nations*, https://www.un.org/sites/un2.un.org/files/un_ai_advisory_body_interim_report_press_release.pdf.
14. Raj Reddy in *Wikipedia*. See the citation of his *Nobel-Prize-equivalent Turing Award (1994)*. Also see: PS Suryanarayana, *Smart Diplomacy: Exploring China-India Synergy* (Hackensack, New Jersey, USA: World Century, 2016), p. 34.
15. Chris Miller, *Chip War: The Fight for the World's Most Critical Technology*, (London: Simon & Schuster, 2022), pp. xvi, 238, 250.
16. A few technical facts in this chapter are from the author's conversations with those familiar with the fast-developing AI situation across the world. Other details are suitably attributed, and the author's analysis and opinions will be self-evident.

17. Qi Haotian, China's Evolving AI Development: Emergent Process Transcending Instrumentalism and Morality, *The AI Wave in Defence Innovation: Assessing Military Artificial Intelligence Strategies, Capabilities, and Trajectories*, Edited by Michael Raska and Richard A. Bitzinger (Oxon and New York: Routledge, 2023), p. 139.
18. Ibid.
19. Ibid, pp. 139-142.
20. "Secretary-General Urges Security Council to Ensure Transparency, Accountability, Oversight, in First Debate on Artificial Intelligence", *UN Press*, https://press.un.org/en/2023/sgsm21880.doc.htm.
21. Cansu Canca, "AI Ethics and Governance in Defence Innovation: Implementing AI Ethics Framework", *The AI Wave in Defence Innovation: Assessing Military Artificial Intelligence Strategies, Capabilities, and Trajectories*, Edited by Michael Raska and Richard A. Bitzinger (Oxon and New York: Routledge, 2023), p. 64.
22. Ibid.
23. "US Department of Defence, DOD Adopts Ethical Principles for Artificial Intelligence", *US Department of Defense*, https://www.defense.gov/News/Releases/Release/Article/2091996/dod-adopts-ethical-principles-for-artificial-intelligence/.
24. Chinese spokespersons' polemical statements against US "hegemony" are too numerous to be missed or referenced.
25. Canca, n.21.
26. To highlight the guidelines of AI-ethical behaviour for the US military personnel, emphasis is suitably added while referencing each of the five categories.
27. Canca, n.21.
28. Pavel Aksenov, "Stanislav Petrov: The man who may have saved the world", *BBC Russian*, https://www.bbc.com/news/world-europe-24280831.
29. Ibid.
30. "Stanislav Petrov, Soviet soldier who saved the world from nuclear Armageddon, dies at 77", *South China Morning Post*, https://www.scmp.com/news/world/russia-central-asia/article/2111810/stanislav-petrov-soviet-soldier-who-saved-world?campaign=2111810&module=perpetual_scroll_0&pgtype=article.
31. "The Man Who "Saved the World" Dies at 77", *Arms Control Association*, https://www.armscontrol.org/act/2017-10/news-briefs/man-saved-world-dies-77.
32. In conversation with this author.
33. In a chat message to this author.

3

India and China: AI Race is Likely

Prime Minister Narendra Modi futurised the India AI Mission, approved on March 7, 2024, as "a giant leap in our [Indian] journey towards becoming a global leader in AI innovation".[1] As evident from this goal, Delhi's primary focus, at this writing, was on joining a potential global elite group of AI-innovating countries in due course. Helming any potential global AI order was not spelt out, directly or indirectly, as India's primary goal.

Modi showed his optimism through a post on twitter (X), "A landmark day for tech and innovation! The [Indian] Cabinet's approval for the IndiaAI Mission will empower AI startups and expand access to compute infrastructure, marking a giant leap in our [Indian] journey towards becoming a global leader in AI innovation".[2]

India's calibrated choice of a niche role in the domain of AI innovation is not the same as the combative approach of the US and China towards each other. They are aggressively vying for global leadership in all domains of any future AI world order. It is argued that there is a distinction between India's journey to become a global leader in the niche domain of AI innovation and global leadership in all the AI domains. Viewed in this perspective, India is messaging that its AI policy is benign globalism with a pragmatic touch.

Delhi's study focused on empowering AI startups, as disclosed by Modi, and was (and can continue to be) a pragmatic approach towards the future. It is driven by India's relatively greater AI resourcefulness rather than financial capital resources. Furthermore, Delhi's objective of "becoming a [not the] global leader in AI innovation" reflects a non-threatening globalism. In another sign of pragmatism laced with non-threatening globalism, India is still "playing catch-up" in AI, as emphasised by External Affairs Minister Dr S. Jaishankar in December 2023. A challenge for India emanates from its neighbour, China, which seeks to deploy its Belt and Road Forum (BRF) to gain a niche role in global AI governance.[3]

India is a conscientious critic of the BRF and its foundational policy, the Belt and Road Initiative (BRI). In Delhi's view, China's strategically motivated investments in its BRF partner states leave them significantly indebted, caught in a debt trap situation – originally described as an unsustainable debt burden.[4] Moreover, Delhi continues to oppose a BRI project called the China-Pakistan Economic Corridor (CPEC), which passes through Pakistan-occupied sovereign Indian territory. China might also spread its AI wings over its BRF partner states in India's neighbourhood. For this and global reasons, India's AI priorities merit serious attention.

The IndiaAI Mission is an aspirational public-private partnership model for five years, with an anticipated funding portfolio of over Rs. 10,000 crores. The aim is to build a robust AI innovation ecosystem. In a bid to become an elite AI-savvy power, India is planning to set up "a cutting-edge, scalable AI computing infrastructure".[5] During the five-year period, over 10,000 Graphics Processing Units (GPUs), the brain-power of hyper-tech AI will be deployed across India, it is officially stated. This initiative, being styled as 'IndiaAI Compute Capacity', is projected as the centrepiece of the entire blueprint.

Other key initiatives under the rubric of the IndiaAI Mission include an Innovation Centre, Datasets Platform, Application (Aps) Development, Future Skills, Startup Financing, and Safe & Trusted AI. The substance of these "initiatives" is evident from their respective terminologies. Of these, the Innovation Centre is envisioned as an academic institution mandated to retain research talent in India and "spearhead the development and deployment" of "indigenous large multimodal models".[6]

To boost innovation and governance, the Mission's Independent Business Division will be tasked to develop the Datasets Platform. Its portfolio is to enhance the "accessibility, quality and utility of public sector datasets". The overall objectives of the IndiaAI Mission are spelt out as "technological self-reliance" and "ethical and responsible AI deployment" besides the "democratisation of AI benefits" for all Indians.[7]

Ahead of the UN Summit of the Future, India, armed with its AI Mission, was aspiring to shape at least the AI innovation and digital technology action plans.[8] In that context, India had not officially spoken of competing with the US and/or China to capture the highest leadership position in any global AI order of the future.

Separately, using empirical research,[9] Harvard Business Review noted, in December 2023, that Washington and Beijing were already waging a "digital cold war" to be "the world's top AI economy".[10] In such a categorical assertion, any future global AI order could be headed by either the US or China.

In this climate of opinion, Modi's optimism in March 2024 climaxed efforts since 2018 when a "brand of AI leadership" was conceptualised as India's potential or likely strategy.[11] Outlined by the National Institution for Transforming India (NITI) Aayog, the brand was not projected as the country's catapult for helming any future pyramid of global AI powers. Instead, NITI Aayog's nuanced strategic aim was for India to become a leading AI power with the capabilities of a benign global mentor.

Reasons for the India-China AI Race

Compare and contrast China's approach with that of India. The do-s and don'ts for all countries, as spelt out in the Chinese "Global AI Governance Initiative" of October 2023, reflected Beijing's updated objectives. First, China aspired to become a global mentor and a great power in hyper-advanced technologies. By then, China had begun to harbour ideas of eventually heading a universal AI order. Thus it can be claimed that a Sino-Indian AI race is likely sooner or later for two reasons.

First, a primary cause is competitive nationalism in the complicated Sino-Indian geostrategic ties. Secondly, India's objective of becoming "a global leader in [just] AI innovation" is a challenge that China might not ignore while seeking to helm a future universal AI order. Such an attitude towards India may animate China even if it has to settle for sharing the global AI leadership with the US. Or remaining second in the pecking order. However, the US and China may not be the only great powers in the AI world of the future. India's credentials and prospects, besides those of some European states, are being recognised internationally. Unveiling an empirical 'scorecard' for 25 top-ranked AI nations, Fletcher School placed India at the 15th position in a list of competitors.[12] The US and China emerged as the

1st- and 2nd-ranked AI powers. The rank of each country was determined by its cumulative score in four domains. Two of these domains featured the AI resources of each country, while two others featured AI resourcefulness. The availability of quality data and the ease of access to such data in each of the 25 countries could be seen as a resource domain. The quality and quantity of AI talent, investments in developing AI and its related technologies, etc., constituted the capital resource. One domain of resourcefulness consisted of rules and/or policies for data governance, including those relating to the localisation and internationalisation of data in each country.

Inevitably, AI innovation was a decisive domain of resourcefulness. Advancements in creating AI models, other creative aspects like AI patents, and research publications and citations in each country were the hallmarks of innovation. With such an ambience prevailing in March 2024, Modi envisioned the newly approved IndiaAI Mission as a giant leap towards the country's aspirational future as a global leader in AI innovation.

What are India's credentials for AI innovation? A clear answer can be traced to the following narrative in the Harvard Business Review: "With strengths across many dimensions, India is the one with greatest upward potential [despite the 15th rank among 25 countries]. It has the largest volume of mobile data consumption and is expected to top the world in data consumption by 2028. It already processes more digital payments than any other country in the world and has the third-largest AI talent pool. While it places restrictions on access to data, its AI regulation rules are still fluid [at about mid-December 2023]. In July, the Telecom Regulatory Authority of India issued a new consultation paper that called for a statutory authority to regulate AI in India through the lens of a 'risk-based framework'. It also suggested collaborating with governments and international agencies to advance the 'responsible use' of AI globally – a process that India could be quite significant in shaping (emphasis added)".[13]

Of particular challenge to China, in its aspirational efforts to become the global AI leader, is this independent assessment that India has the greatest upward potential. A Sino-Indian AI race is entirely conceivable in these circumstances. However, this race need not be a zero-sum game. China seeks to lead and guide countries at the helm of global affairs in AI. India is pursuing a calibrated path upwards, beginning with AI innovation. It is possible, therefore, that the race between India and China may centre on the core issue of AI innovation, at least for a start.

Synchronous with this situation, India's priorities for the UN Summit of the Future – in cyber-digital and AI domains – were outlined in January 2024 within a framework of inter-governmental negotiations. Under UN auspices, 'A Pact for the Future' was already being negotiated through the inter-governmental process involving India as well. Yet, going by the relevant document on India's priorities, there was no attempt by India at unilateralism to influence the outcome of the global summit.[14]

India has, of course, associated itself with partners in the Quad[15] on issues of AI. Whereas China signalled its ambition to orchestrate BRF's bloc thinking about AI, India does not seek to impose its AI perspective on the Quad. Consultative dialogue has remained the primary practice in the Quad, although the US often leads in setting the agenda. India, for its part, appears to recognise the importance of US initiatives in the Quad.

In a relevant context, Prime Minister Narendra Modi had, twice in 2023, brought together more than 100 disparate developing countries known as the Global South. His objective was to sensitise the Group of Twenty (G20) major economies to the Global South's old and new development concerns.[16]

Despite such a pursuit as the then G20 president, India did not try to impose its own or Global South's perspective at the two G20 summits in Delhi in 2023. Neither did India do so at the preceding Quad summit in Hiroshima (also in 2023), although India had already organised a 'Voice of the Global South' online summit. In December 2023, Modi told the Global Partnership on AI (GPAI) summit that G20 had, in September, accepted the principle of "ethical use of AI".[17] This acceptance was not the result of any imposition by the then G20 president, India because the principle was already an international mantra in the AI circles.

On a different geostrategic track, Modi and US President Joe Biden had announced, in May 2022, an exclusive US-India Initiative on Critical and Emerging Technologies (iCET).[18] The iCET took off in January 2023.[19] Furthermore, after meeting Modi at the White House on June 22, of the same year, Biden said, "We're unlocking a shared future" of "unlimited potential". An aspect of the potential collaboration that Biden identified was "harnessing our shared expertise" on "quantum computing and AI".[20] The future trajectory of this potential US-India high-tech collaboration will be watched closely by the international community, particularly by China.

High-Tech Candour

In December 2023, Jaishankar was indeed candid in assessing India's role and relevance in high-tech matters. In brief, his overarching perspective: "We're playing catch-up because while our era of reform started three decades ago, the era of reform was not necessarily the era of technology. We conceptualised reform in much narrower terms... a lot of it ended up in very narrowly defined economics, much of it centred around trade and, to some degree, investment".[21] By being less categorical – the "era of reform was not necessarily the era of technology" – Jaishankar seemed to acknowledge the progress made by the country in the 20th century. During Prime Minister Jawaharlal Nehru's first term, technology education, space and civil nuclear energy programmes were initiated. India made some rapid strides during the terms of three later prime ministers in the 20th century – Indira Gandhi, Rajiv Gandhi, and PV Narasimha Rao. The key technological domains where progress was made then were nuclear weaponisation, telecommunications and space (especially regarding cryogenic engines).

On balance, however, Jaishankar's argument appeared to be two-pronged: India had finally entered an era of technology under Prime Minister Narendra Modi's watch, and the country would need to stay the course and also forge ahead.

About AI, Jaishankar was much more forthright: "At the moment, of course, one particular area of interest is the debate about responsible AI... when it comes to technology, today the challenge, as it is in much of international relations, is how to compete, but how to compete with responsibility".[22]

India's situation of having to compete with several countries, notably China, is very real indeed, especially in the perceivable futurist AI domain. This is so because China, as seen from Delhi, resorts to grey-zone tactics of exerting pressure (or coercion) below the red line of full-scale war in many fields.[23] Suspicion has centred on China as the source of some AI-enabled cyber-attacks in India, not just in the US, which assertively chronicles such attacks on it.

China's "massive investment in AI development" and "integration into the global high-tech supply chain" will test India's "techplomacy", according to Shashi Shekhar Vempati, a writer on AI geopolitics. Creative avenues open to India's techplomacy would be "engaging with China and countering potential harm from its actions". In coping with "China's AI rise", Delhi's "diplomatic agenda around AI" should "ideally involve international cooperation, healthy competition and strategic containment", he has proposed.[24]

AI Strategy of India

As already noted, the NITI Aayog had, in June 2018, outlined the "national strategy for AI" – an "approach to leadership in AI". Sighting a goalpost, NITI Aayog significantly noted as follows: "The truly transformative nature of the technology, yet the nascent stage of its adoption worldwide, provide India with an opportunity to define its own brand of AI leadership". For India, its "own brand of AI leadership", evidently worldwide, continues to be this particular goalpost while seeking to seize the "opportunity" to reach there through policies and performance.

In NITI Aayog's view, India "should", under its "national strategy" of "AI for All", "leverage AI" primarily for inclusive economic growth and social development at home. The "proposed" Indian "brand" of "AI for All" "should ... finally" serve as a "garage for emerging and developing economies", NITI Aayog recommended.[25] This aspect of becoming a model AI "garage" – for the benefit of disparate developing countries of the Global South – seems to be India's more immediate aim. An essential step in this regard was announced in 2023.

Unsurprising in this light was the Indian Finance Ministry's reported offer in 2023 to allow foreign countries and their corporations to set up 'data embassies' in India. Those responding to such an offer would enjoy 'diplomatic immunity' for their digital data that might be stored in India. In quid pro quo, Indian data could be stored in a foreign cloud under India's laws if foreign data were parked in India under the relevant foreign laws.[26]

Such an Indian outreach towards foreign countries was not a hegemonic unilateral effort to set a universal AI agenda, norms and standards. The reason was simple but significant. Unlike the suspicion about China's unilateral hegemonic efforts, India had not floated any flamboyant global initiative for AI governance.

However, Delhi is unlikely to be a bystander at the United Nations, Quad, or G20 whenever it seeks to set a global or regional AI agenda. India is the "largest digitally connected democracy", officially with at least 830 million internet users as of May 2023.[27] It is reasonable, therefore, that India must have a key place at any future high table on AI matters at the global level.

Unlike China's plans to globalise its AI and contribute to the world as a key AI superpower, India's National Strategy for AI has not alarmed any major power. Societal needs within India were identified by NITI Aayog for deploying AI capabilities. Health care, agriculture, education, smart cities and infrastructure, as well as smart mobility and transportation, were projected as the best AI-injectable sectors in India.

NITI Aayog had suggested fostering capabilities in core and applied AI research, access to intelligent data, and fairness, accountability and transparency in data usage for training and deploying AI models. The Indian government, it was emphasised, has to play the critical role of a catalyst to ensure robust intellectual property protection and adopt international standards across the AI ecosystem.

According to NITI Aayog, the overall objective is to "ensure for India its rightful place in this [AI] transformational era".[28] In a Status Paper in August 2020, the Future Networks Division of Indian Government's Telecommunications Engineering Centre (ITEC) focused its attention on the imperative of AI inventions. ITEC noted as follows: "India is amongst the top 3 largest startup hubs of the world. A national programme on AI shall catalyse these innovative minds to co-create [AI] solutions... The country should also create targeted datasets and incubation hubs for startups".[29]

Taking a deeper look at India's AI strategy in October 2023, the Software Freedom Law Centre, too, focused on the imperative of India's own AI inventions: "In India, non-resident Indians (NRIs) file [applications for] more patents than residents, while also receiving more patents. This suggests that a significant portion of AI patent ownership is foreign [-based]... Further, there is an urgent need to adopt Free and Open-Source Software (FOSS) in publicly funded research... Using open source and open innovation models can boost inventive activity".[30]

India's national AI programme, reported[31] in January 2024, was expected to place the country in the elite AI Club, consisting of the US and China, among a few others. Referring to this programme, a Carnegie India commentary in February noted that Delhi's "proposed light-touch approach to AI regulation is likely to resonate with countries in the Global South".[32] On March 7, 2024, this programme, officially known as IndiaAI Mission, was approved, with Modi hailing it for its potential to make India a global leader in AI innovation.[33]

AI Strategy of China

China's AI ambitions are no secret, with the State Council having issued the New Generation Artificial Intelligence Development Plan (AIDP) in 2017. This plan was designed to make China a global innovation centre by 2030. The Council stipulated that the value of the cumulative output of Chinese AI industries should, therefore, exceed US $150 billion by 2030.

Under this AIDP, another key aim was to ensure that Chinese AI would "contribute to the world".[34] This particular aim, if decoded on the basis of the plan's overall framework, was that China should become a key AI superpower. AI should also help promote China's technology, economy, social welfare and security, the Council said.

The AIDP also envisioned Chinese breakthroughs in big data intelligence, multimedia-aware computing, human-machine hybrid intelligence, swarm intelligence, and automated decision-making. Mandated by the State Council was research in some advanced areas such as brain-like computing, quantum intelligence computing and higher levels of machine learning. The development of an integrated technology system – harmonised use of data, algorithms and hardware – was also recommended for China.

Urging the mainstreaming of human-machine collaboration, the Chinese State Council called for the promotion of the AI economy – an ecosystem of new industries, all powered by this hyper-advanced technology. Smart robots, smart vehicles, virtual reality, augmented reality, smart terminals, etc., would populate the AI economy, the State Council said. AI technology should also be applied to drive even the traditional industries, it was further advised. In a punchline of the AIDP, Beijing indicated its intentions to create a fund for AI promotion and to apply AI to China's national defence as well.[35]

Separately, a goal under the Chinese State Council's Made in China 2025 plan is "to achieve indigenous AI capabilities to match or even surpass the West".[36] To boost the morale of Chinese AI specialists in that context, the Council alerted them to recognise that AI "has become a new focal point of international competition". Major powers were already developing their indigenous AI capabilities to "enhance national competitiveness and protect national security", the Council warned Chinese AI specialists. The Chinese State Council's observations show that, in this era of hyper-advanced technologies, Beijing must seek AI-enabled national security and the coveted role of a major AI superpower.[37]

In a substantive word-play on a ubiquitous catchphrase in Beijing's discourse, author Jinghan Zeng has sought to lay bare the nuances of AI with Chinese characteristics. Reviewing this 2022 book, Ian Forsyth has written as follows: "Zeng first argues that... China's AI 'strategy' is more of a political manifesto than a concrete policy plan... AI is part of a digital technology package that the Chinese Communist Party has actively employed to not only improve public services but also to strengthen domestic control and become a global technological leader. Zeng warns that this could result in proving the ideological superiority of its authoritarian and communist values".[38]

India's AI 'Doctrine'

While India and China have not formally announced their respective AI doctrine, Beijing revealed its principles and preferences in its Global AI Governance Initiative. Some aspects of India's principles were disclosed in its priorities for the 78th session of the UN General Assembly ahead of the September 2024 Summit of the Future. India, unlike China, did not appear eager to set unilateral norms without waiting for that summit's outcome.

The focal point of India's AI-related diplomacy, as discernible from the priorities, was (and is) an inclusive digital economy"[39] covering all countries. To ensure "a digital future for all", Delhi would like "technology transfer" from the advanced high-tech powers to the countries in need of the relevant know-how. Closely related to this principle is the idea of externally-aided capacity building of the states that have inadequate digital know-how and infrastructure.

In Delhi's overarching perspective, the "digital future for all" should be "inclusive, equitable and sustainable". In this context, the inclusive attribute denotes digital benefits for all countries. An equitable digital future will ensure fairness and transparency in the delivery of benefits. A sustainable future is one that would last long on the basis of interdependence among all countries. The key beneficiaries of a sustainable future, in terms of high-tech-aided economic development, should be the Global South. This composite interpretation of different strands of the "digital future for all" is pure common sense.

India's calibrated focus on AI as a characteristic of the "digital future for all" seems a practical necessity due to the unpredictable evolution of this amazing technology.[40] From this perspective, it would be a mistake, though, to think that AI is an afterthought in India's "priorities" for a universal digital order.

Arguably, India's other priorities designed to ensure an "inclusive, equitable and sustainable" global digital order are well-known. These are a universal internet without fragmentation, investments for the required connectivity through infrastructures, non-discriminatory access to networks and, above all, data protection to preserve civilised freedoms.

Clearly evident from this dense discussion are the early signs of India's emerging AI doctrine. Non-threatening globalism, flowing from a categorical emphasis on AI innovation, constitutes the crux of Delhi's evolving AI 'doctrine'. As for the likely or potential military aspects of such a doctrine, India has set for itself two interrelated goals. These are strategic edge over the adversary to constantly ensure India's AI capabilities for deterrence (discussed in Chapter 1).

China's AI 'Doctrine'

In contrast to Delhi's approach, Beijing's "Global AI Governance Initiative" was unveiled in October 2023 as the apparent consensus within a China-led bloc – BRF.[41] For Chinese diplomacy, as noted before, the BRF is not an ideological bloc but a concert of economies. Nonetheless, unmistakable was China's aim to set norms for AI, almost a year before the UN Summit of the Future, without waiting for any global consensus.[42] Surely, this is a sign of the Chinese aspiration to become a global AI superpower or even helm a worldwide AI order in due course.

Five strands of the Chinese principles for global AI governance stand out in a multi-point initiative on behalf of a multilateral bloc. These are (1) respect for national sovereignty; (2) respect for the relevant international laws; (3) the creation of trustworthy AI technologies that could be reviewed, monitored and traced; (4) human control over AI capabilities at all times; and (5) prudent and responsible attitude to the research, development, and application of AI technologies in the military field (emphasis added).

Beijing expressed support for "discussions within the United Nations framework to establish an international institution to govern AI".[43] This significant offer, sure to resonate in the UN circles, was arguably meant to address concerns about China's attempts at unilateral consensus-building on this high-tech issue.

The always-China-led BRF was hailed by China itself in December 2023 as "the world's most broad-based and largest platform for international cooperation". The BRF was also projected as "the platform for action" to implement "the core tenet of Xi Jinping Thought on Diplomacy" – "a shared future for mankind".[44]

Evident from various strands of the "Global AI Governance Initiative" is a hierarchy of China's principles. Let us try to harmonise respect for the universally understood concept of national sovereignty with the undefined idea of "a shared future for mankind". Under the resulting AI 'doctrine', China might insist on exercising its sovereignty as a global leader or hegemon and seek to shape the shared future of all countries. Time alone will tell, as monopolistic control of AI by any single country is quite unlikely at this writing.

High-Tech 'Bloc Thinking'

If, as it seems, China is leading the BRF bloc (with or without some dissonance among the members), does India lead and/or belong to any significant bloc? There is a conceptual attempt in the West to include India in a proposed informal coalition (or bloc) of techno-democracies to face the perceived challenge from China-led techno-autocracies.[45]

This idea, floated by Jared Cohen and Richard Fontaine[46] on building digital cooperation, resonates in the Western discourse on the unfolding saga of cyber-digital and AI technologies. China, now an American peer in technology, is seen to be at the forefront of autocratic states.[47]

Moreover, as Jinghan Zeng has argued, AI is, for China, a blend of advanced technology laced with political ideology. The Chinese political ideology of autocracy is basically a system in which the leader is said to know best on all matters of state. In contrast, India has a "strategic technology partnership"[48] with the US. Both India and the US share a common political ideology of democracy, but their potential technological partnership is essentially a strategic choice to face China.[49]

Look at contra scenarios as well. China[50] and the United States[51] (US) were willing, in this writing, to discuss bilateral AI cooperation. For the Chinese, such cooperation could, in one scenario, lead to joint Sino-American AI leadership globally. Nonetheless, Beijing had already deployed its BRF as a springboard for China's solo AI leadership in a multilateral (eventually, global) setting.[52]

For Beijing, this gambit could be a bargaining chip in talks with the US. Or, more simply, a fallback position should Washington resist any idea of a potential joint AI leadership. From this author's perspective, China might even seek solo or exclusive global leadership by trying to outsmart the US in the proposed bilateral AI talks. This would be in line with the legacy of China's ancient strategist, Sun Tzu.

Inaugurating the third BRF conference in Beijing in October 2023, Chinese President Xi Jinping said his country would put forward at that forum a global initiative for AI governance.[53] China did present, at that conference itself, a unilateral initiative for worldwide governance of AI.[54] Evident, therefore, on that occasion were Xi's orchestration of BRF's bloc thinking and BRF's support for a China-led global AI order.

Beijing had also projected the BRF as a group of countries linked to China – a concert of economies[55] (not an ideological bloc) as with the Asian Infrastructure Investment Bank. At the BRF, therefore, Xi sought to influence the September 2024 UN Summit of the Future without waiting for the world's premier institution to evolve a truly global AI initiative. Despite such tactical and strategic considerations, Beijing cannot wish away Washington and Delhi in the current and futurist AI scenarios.

In the potential Sino-Indian AI race, therefore, India may have the option of seeking meaningful technological cooperation with the advanced US. However, China may not be able to bank on cooperation with an advanced technological power, especially if India keeps its ties with Russia in reasonably good condition. However, it is too early to predict the global technology battle lines, with no country in full control of AI, which has almost attained the (metaphoric) escape velocity. The geopolitics of control over this grey zone of AI is just beginning.

Notes

1. Narendra Modi, "Cabinet Approves Ambitious IndiaAI Mission to Strengthen the AI Innovation Ecosystem", *Narendra Modi*, https://www.narendramodi.in/cabinet-approves-ambitious-indiaai-mission-to-strengthen-the-ai-innovation-ecosystem-580269.
2. Ibid.

3. Xi Jinping, "Building an Open, Inclusive and Interconnected World for Common Development", *Belt and Road Forum for International Cooperation*, http://www.beltandroadforum.org/english/n101/2023/1018/c124-1175.html.
4. "Official Spokesperson's response to a query on participation of India in OBOR/BRI Forum", *Ministry of External Affairs*, Government of India, https://www.mea.gov.in/media-briefings.htm?dtl/28463/Official+Spokespersons+response+to+a+query+on+participation+of+India+in+OBORBRI+Forum.
5. "Cabinet Approves Over Rs 10,300 Crore for IndiaAI Mission, will Empower AI Startups and Expand Compute Infrastructure Access," *Ministry of Electronics & IT*, https://pib.gov.in/PressReleasePage.aspx?PRID=2012375.
6. Ibid.
7. Ibid.
8. "Priorities for the 78th Session of the United Nations General Assembly", *Ministry of External Affairs*, GoI, https://www.mea.gov.in/india-priorities-unga.htm.
9. "The Emerging Geography of AI: Introducing the Top-Ranked AI Nations (TRAIN) Scorecard", *Digital Planet*, Fletcher School, Tufts University (US), https://digitalplanet.tufts.edu/the-emerging-geography-of-ai/.
10. Bhaskar Chakravorti, Ajay Bhalla and Ravi Shankar Chaturvedi, "Charting the Emerging Geography of AI", *Harvard Business Review*, https://hbr.org/2023/12/charting-the-emerging-geography-of-ai.
11. "National Strategy for Artificial Intelligence", *NITI Aayog*, https://www.niti.gov.in/sites/default/files/2023-03/National-Strategy-for-Artificial-Intelligence.pdf.
12. n.9.
13. n.10.
14. n.8.
15. Quad is an Indo-Pacific security dialogue forum comprising the US, Japan, India, and Australia.
16. "Summary of Deliberations: Voice of Global South Summit 2023 (January 12-13, 2023)", Ministry fo External Affairs, https://www.mea.gov.in/bilateral-documents.htm?dtl/36119.
17. "English rendering of PM's address at the inauguration of GPAI Summit, 2023", *Prime Minister's Office*, https://pib.gov.in/PressReleasePage.aspx?PRID=1985614.
18. "FACT SHEET: United States and India Elevate Strategic Partnership with the initiative on Critical and Emerging Technology (iCET)", *The White House*, https://www.whitehouse.gov/briefing-room/statements-releases/2023/01/31/fact-sheet-united-states-and-india-elevate-strategic-partnership-with-the-initiative-on-critical-and-emerging-technology-icet/.
19. Ibid.
20. "Remarks by President Biden and Prime Minister Modi of the Republic of India in Joint Press Conference", *The White House*, https://www.whitehouse.gov/briefing-

room/speeches-remarks/2023/06/22/remarks-by-president-biden-and-prime-minister-modi-of-the-republic-of-india-in-joint-press-conference/.

21. Dr S. Jaishankar, "Inaugural Address by EAM, Dr. S. Jaishankar at the Global Technology Summit", Ministry of External Affairs, https://www.mea.gov.in/speeches-statements.htm?dtl/37337/inaugural_address_by_eam_dr_s_jaishankar_at_the_global_technology_summit.
22. Ibid.
23. Vijay Gokhale, "Review of Ketian Zhang's *China's Gambit — The Calculus of Coercion*: Message from the Mainland", *The Hindu*, https://www.thehindu.com/books/books-reviews/a-book-for-the-indian-strategic-community-as-it-ponders-over-how-to-deal-with-china-in-2024/article67837612.ece). Also see: P S Suryanarayana, "China-India Rivalry: The Saga of Game Changers", *East Asian Policy: an international quarterly*, Vol. 13, No. 2, April/June 2021, pp. 5—18.
24. Shashi Shekhar Vempati, "India's Opportunity to Show the Way on Artificial Intelligence for Greater Global Good", *Emerging Technologies and Indian Diplomacy*, Indian Council of World Affairs, New Delhi, January 2024, https://icwa.in/pdfs/EmergingTechnologiesIndianDiplomacyweb.pdf.
25. n.11.
26. The reported Indian proposal of "data embassies" is cited from "The Key Policy Frameworks Governing AI in India", *Access Partnership*, https://accesspartnership.com/the-key-policy-frameworks-governing-ai-in-india/.
27. "MoS Rajeev Chandrasekhar to hold a Digital India Dialogues' session tomorrow in Mumbai on principles of Digital India Act", *Ministry of Electronics & IT*, https://pib.gov.in/PressReleseDetailm.aspx?PRID=1926443#:~:text=India%20today%20has%20830%20million,largest%20%E2%80%9Cdigitally%20connected%20democracy%E2%80%9D.
28. n.11.
29. "AI Policies in India A status Paper", *Telecommunications Engineering Centre*, https://www.tec.gov.in/pdf/Studypaper/AI%20Policies%20in%20India%20A%20status%20Paper%20final.pdf.
30. "The Indian Strategy on AI: A Deeper Look", *Software Freedom Law Center*, https://sflc.in/the-indian-strategy-on-ai-a-deeper-look/#:~:text=India%27s%20AI%20strategy%20undertakes%20a,data%20interoperability%2C%20and%20legal%20frameworks.
31. "India ai programme: Meity to seek Cabinet nod for India AI programme entailing over Rs 10,000 crore investments: MoS IT", *The Economic Times*, https://economictimes.indiatimes.com/tech/technology/meity-to-seek-cabinet-nod-for-india-ai-programme-entailing-over-rs-10000-crore-investments-mos-it/articleshow/107099413.cms?from=mdr.

32. Amlan Mohanty, Shatakratu Sahu, "India's AI Strategy: Balancing Risk and Opportunity" *Carnegie India*; https://carnegieindia.org/2024/02/22/india-s-ai-strategy-balancing-risk-and-opportunity-pub-91693.
33. n.1.
34. "China issues guideline on artificial intelligence development", *State Council*, PRC, https://english.www.gov.cn/policies/latest_releases/2017/07/20/content_281475742458322.htm.
35. Ibid.
36. Qi Haotian, "China's Evolving AI Development: Emergent Process Transcending Instrumentalism and Morality", *The AI Wave in Defence Innovation: Assessing Military Artificial Intelligence Strategies, Capabilities, and Trajectories*, Edited by Michael Raska and Richard A. Bitzinger (Oxon and New York: Routledge, 2023), p. 138.
37. This author's inference from the Chinese State Council's AIDP.
38. Jinghan Zeng, *Artificial Intelligence with Chinese Characteristics: National Strategy, Security and Authoritarian Governance* (Singapore: Palgrave Macmillan Press, 2022) (Book review by Ian Forsyth, *Journal of Indo-Pacific Affairs*, July 2022).
39. n.8.
40. Ibid.
41. "Global AI Governance Initiative", *Belt and Road Forum*, http://www.beltandroadforum.org/english/n101/2023/1019/c127-1231.html.
42. This author's interpretation of China's "Global AI Governance Initiative".
43. n.41.
44. "The Central Conference on Work Relating to Foreign Affairs was Held in Beijing Xi Jinping Delivered an Important Address at the Conference", *Ministry of Foreign Affairs*, PRC, https://www.fmprc.gov.cn/eng/zxxx_662805/202312/t20231228_11214416.html (Last accessed on February 25, 2024).
45. Anu Bradford, *Digital Empires: The Global Battle to Regulate Technology* (USA: Oxford University Press, 2023), p. 389.
46. Jared Cohen, Richard Fontaine, "How Cooperating on Digital Technology Can Unite Democracies", *Foreign Affairs*, November/December 2020, https://www.foreignaffairs.com/articles/united-states/2020-10-13/uniting-techno-democracies
47. Ibid.
48. "Remarks by President Biden and Prime Minister Modi of the Republic of India in Joint Press Conference", *The White House*, https://www.whitehouse.gov/briefing-room/speeches-remarks/2023/06/22/remarks-by-president-biden-and-prime-minister-modi-of-the-republic-of-india-in-joint-press-conference/.
49. This author's interpretation.
50. Chinese Ambassador to the US Xie Feng, "Speech by Chinese Ambassador to the United States Xie Feng at the Carter Center Forum commemorating the 45th

anniversary of the establishment of China-U.S. relations" https://www.fmprc.gov.cn/eng/wjb_663304/zwjg_665342/zwbd_665378/202401/t20240111_11221867.html.

51. "Readout of President Joe Biden's Meeting with President Xi Jinping of the People's Republic of China", The White House, https://www.whitehouse.gov/briefing-room/statements-releases/2023/11/15/readout-of-president-joe-bidens-meeting-with-president-xi-jinping-of-the-peoples-republic-of-china-2/.
52. This author's interpretation based on participation as a delegate in the inaugural Belt and Road Forum (BRF) in Beijing in May 2017, besides interactions with Chinese diplomats over a number of years. The same applies to the interpretation of likely Chinese strategy during any serious US-China bilateral dialogue on AI – especially after China's "Global AI Governance Initiative" was launched at the Third BRF meeting in October 2023.
53. n.3.
54. "Global AI Governance Initiative--The Third Belt and Road Forum for International Cooperation", *Belt and Road Forum*, http://www.beltandroadforum.org/english/n101/2023/1019/c127-1231.html.
55. Suryanarayana, *The Elusive Tipping Point: China-India Ties for a New Order* (Singapore: World Scientific, 2021), pp. 225, 226 and 236.

4

AI Arms: Calculus of Power and Principles

Leaders of nation-states often seek to defeat their external adversaries by developing new weapons of war or procuring them from other states for deployment and use. The latest force multipliers, gradually coming into vogue in the first quarter of the 21st century, are weapons powered by artificial intelligence (AI). Among these are the state-of-the-art AI Lethal Autonomous Weapons Systems (AI-LAWS) under varying degrees of human control.

The elevated global concern, at this writing, is that AI-LAWS, without any human control at all, might become weapons of choice sooner than later in the foreseeable future. This could become an existential threat to some or all countries.

Autonomy is the essential characteristic of AI-LAWS. Depending on the strategic objectives of states (and, perhaps, non-state actors, too) who might develop, deploy and use such weapons, the nature and scope of autonomy will be determined.

A "Political Declaration on Responsible Military Use of Artificial Intelligence and Autonomy", issued by the US State Department on November 9, 2023, outlined AI-powered autonomy as follows: "Artificial Intelligence may be understood to refer to the ability of machines to perform tasks that would otherwise require human intelligence... An AI application could guide or change the behaviour of an autonomous physical [weapon] system or perform tasks that remain purely in the digital realm. Autonomy may be understood as a spectrum and [may be understood] to involve a [weapon] system operating without further human intervention after activation".[1]

In the strategic thought from ancient to the current post-modern times, human desire for state-of-the-art weapons of war has been a critical aspect of power calculus. As a principle of military statecraft, the acquisition and use of lethal tech-driven weapons, always under human control, acquired legitimacy in the international affairs of past eras.

A crucial difference for the foreseeable future, though, is the ethical principle of salvaging the seemingly endangered absolute human control over any state's AI-LAWS in the military domain. Another major concern is that non-state actors like militants or terrorists might also seek and obtain LAWS driven by AI without human control.

The absence or loss of human control over AI-LAWS could be seen as a violation of the existing and future International Humanitarian Law (IHL). The International Committee of the Red Cross (ICRC) has summarised IHL, or "rules of war", as follows: "IHL regulates how wars are fought, balancing two aspects: weakening the enemy and limiting suffering". The "main purpose ... is to maintain some [sense of] humanity in armed conflicts, saving lives and reducing suffering".[2]

With 196 states having ratified the relevant Geneva Conventions, rules of war acquired universality. In this light, the imperative of human control over AI-LAWS was championed by Guterres ahead of the September 2024 UN Summit of the Future. As noted in Chapter 2, speaking in July 2023, he advocated for the "prohibition of [those] lethal autonomous weapons [which are deployable] without human control".[3]

AI and Emotional Intelligence

In June 1977, the original law of Geneva, on protecting victims of armed conflict, was combined with the law of The Hague on rights and obligations of belligerents. Such a composite IHL remains in vogue at this writing. The overarching mandate was (and is) to limit the "legitimate purpose of a conflict". According to ICRC, the "legitimate purpose" would be "the complete or partial submission of the enemy at the earliest possible moment with the minimum expenditure of life and resources".[4]

Evident from these basic tenets of rules of war is the absolute necessity of human judgment in a conflict situation. The idea of protecting lives, even while seeking the submission of the enemy in a war, is an apparent contradiction or, at least, a complex puzzle. A blend of emotional intelligence and rational thinking will be indispensable to observe the Geneva Conventions, therefore, in letter and spirit in this AI age.[5]

Blended human judgment is best suited to resolve the moral-strategic puzzle of post-modern wars. Indeed, a 'deeply learned' but unguided AI machine and the absolutely autonomous state-of-the-art robot, both driven by AI, will be bereft of the required emotional intelligence. This reality, as at the stage of AI evolution before the September 2024 UN Summit of the Future, might not be easily addressed.

However, AI gurus may remain confident about its technological efficacy in the future. Tracing the evolving military deployments of AI, two researchers draw attention to the US Air Force's successful demonstration of human-machine teaming in 2019.[6]

The relevant concept centres on the loyal wingman – an autonomous drone flying alongside a fighter jet to augment the latter's capabilities at the risk of attracting enemy fire. Even in the context of such teaming, a level of human oversight on autonomous AI military systems is a reality. In fact, AI-LAWS "with total freedom over the selection and engagement of targets, are not yet fielded", according to the two researchers.[7]

India's Call for Military-Moral Balance

Although AI-LAWS, without any human control, were not in military deployment anywhere by 2023, the United Nations General Assembly's (UNGA's) First Committee began to fast-track diplomacy to avert danger. On November 1, 2023, the Committee adopted a resolution emphasising "the urgent need for the international community to address the challenges and concerns raised by autonomous weapons systems".

With AI-LAWS potentially becoming a key component of advanced military arsenals worldwide, the Committee wanted to know the "humanitarian, legal, security, technological and ethical perspectives" of all UN members.[8] The UNGA's First Committee deals with disarmament and international security issues.

Significantly, India and Russia, besides three others, voted against this resolution.[9] China was among the eight countries which abstained from voting. The whole issue was so sensitive that the resolution was adopted only after 11 separate recorded votes failed to produce the required majority.

As reported by the UN Press, some members aired two observations reflecting the sensitivities after the final voting. One comment was that "an algorithm must not be in full control of decisions that involve killing or harming humans". The plea to deprive algorithms of full control was a call to preserve human control over AI-LAWS.

Another comment was that "even if an algorithm can determine what is legal under international humanitarian law, it can never determine what is ethical".[10] This comment was in line with ICRC's norms of IHL.

What was India's rationale for voting against the UNGA First Committee's AI arms resolution? In a post-voting explanation, India emphasised its preference for "striking a balance between military necessity and humanitarian imperatives".[11] This principle could be achieved, in Delhi's view, through further discussions in the existing Group of Governmental Experts (GGE) on emerging technologies relating to LAWS.

India had already taken the same position at a GGE meeting on March 6, 2023, calling for "striking a balance between military necessity and humanitarian imperatives".[12] At that GGE meeting, Delhi supported the idea of a high-level political declaration under UN auspices to control AI-LAWS suitably.

The GGE, not the same as the UNGA First Committee, functions under the already-established framework of the UN Convention on Certain Conventional Weapons, and also considers the impact of LAWS. The UNGA First Committee's AI arms resolution would, therefore, result in "a duplication of efforts and resources", India said after the voting ended on November 1.[13]

Delhi's National and Global Concerns

A procedural flaw in the AI arms resolution was also unacceptable to India. Opposing the now-elevated "emphasis on [the] lethal [potentiality]" of AI-LAWS, Delhi pointed out that the GGE was already seized of this matter. A significant strategic flaw was the new "referencing [of] concepts on which there is no [UN-wide] agreement, let alone consensus, such as regional stability".[14] This particular remark flowed from India's opposition to being treated as a simple South Asian regional power. China and Pakistan have often called for unilateral Indian initiatives to ensure regional stability in South Asia by expecting Delhi to ignore its own concerns about the Sino-Pakistani links. Delhi opposes the perceived attempts to confine it to regional geopolitics in disregard of India's overall strategic interests with reference to China's anti-India patronage of Pakistan.

Beyond this interpretation of the China factor in South Asia are the globalised nuances of India's strategic calculus in opposing the resolution. It would be incorrect to conclude that Delhi was somehow against the universal principles that were bandied. Delhi was not known to favour any idea of giving up human control over AI algorithms in a conflict situation.

India had told the GGE session in August 2021 that LAWS must be compliant with the International Humanitarian Law and "must not be uncontrollable".[15] Autonomy of weapons like LAWS was only meant to "impart more precision and accuracy" and to "avoid human errors".[16] At the UNGA in November-December 2023, India's arguments were thus consistent with its previous positions during the GGE sessions on LAWS in August 2021 and March 2023.

In addition, at the UNGA in November-December 2023, India did not see human control over lethal algorithms as the only strategic means to achieve global stability. Or, indeed, to prevent arms races and proliferation. Maintenance of global and regional stability, prevention of arms races, and proliferation were the objectives of some supporters of the UNGA's AI arms resolution. For those supporters, human control over AI-LAWS would be the best means to achieve these objectives.

Perceivable, although unstated in the relevant explanation of the vote, India prefers its own military-deterrence capabilities and a thorough reform of the UNSC to ensure global stability. However, a bleak prospect of reforming the UNSC of 1945 vintage stares humanity in the face at this writing.

National, Bilateral and Multilateral Paths

For China, its Global AI Governance Initiative, unveiled nearly two weeks before the UNGA First Committee's voting, was already the main benchmark. This could explain the Chinese delegation's abstention. As a proactive AI deployer, China was not going to constrain itself by supporting or opposing any norms (outside its own benchmark) in a hurry at that stage.

AI-savvy India, too, appeared to have valued its own national AI strategy as a key benchmark to go by.[17] India and China might have also reckoned that the best occasion for definitive national positions on the capabilities of AI would be the September 2024 Summit of the Future.

Preparing the ground for that Summit, the UNGA adopted its First Committee's resolution at a plenary session on December 22, 2023. Detailing a miscellany of issues, UN Press reported that the UNGA resolution on lethal autonomous weapons systems was adopted by a vote of 152 in favour to 4 against. India and Russia were identified among the four no-sayers, whereas the US supported the resolution of AI arms.[18] China and ten others abstained from voting. The pattern of voting and the nuances thereof were the same as during the voting in the UNGA's First Committee on November 1, 2023.

The adoption of this resolution during the UNGA's plenary session on December 22, 2023, was hailed in some media circles as a facilitator of international rulemaking on 'killer AI'.[19] The US, Japan and other members of the Group of Seven (G7) industrialised countries supported this non-binding UNGA resolution. The only commonality between Washington and Beijing on that occasion was seen to be their possession of advanced military AI technology.

India was depicted as an aspiring power "actively [engaged in] promoting the military use of AI".[20] In such a climate of opinion, India had, in the UNGA's First Committee in November 2023, remarkably advocated for "striking a balance between military necessity and humanitarian imperatives".

The message was that India would not like AI-LAWS to breach the red line of war crimes. Furthermore, on December 12, 2023, Prime Minister Narendra Modi expressed India's overarching commitment to 'Responsible Human-Centric AI'. He did so before the AI arms resolution was adopted by the UNGA at its plenary session on December 22, 2023. Addressing the Global Partnership on Artificial Intelligence (GPAI) summit, Modi said that the Group of Twenty (G20) major economies had agreed on the imperative of "ethical use of AI".[21] The G20 – which includes AI powers like the US, China, Russia and the European Union, besides India – agreed on the ethical use of AI under India's presidency of the group.

AI Arms and US-India Strategic Tech Ties

India's vote against the UNGA's AI arms resolution in November-December 2023 apparently attracted greater international attention than China's agnostic abstention. Mainly because Delhi is widely seen to be 'allied' with Washington, in all but name, through a strategic technology partnership, they also pursue an exclusive bilateral Initiative on Critical and Emerging Technologies (iCET), including AI.[22] However, India, unlike the US, voted against the UNGA's AI arms resolution.

In May 2023, the US and India commenced a new series of Advanced Domains Defence Dialogue (AD3) with emphasis on space and AI.[23] Noteworthy, they discussed "priorities for maintaining safety [and] stability [of technologies], and [priorities for] promoting responsible uses of technologies in these [defence] domains".[24] Despite iCET and AD3, "there is no evidence ... that India has partnered with [any] particular countries [including the US especially] to acquire specific defence AI capabilities".[25] Until this is written, the absence of US-India collaboration in the actual development and deployment of AI arms is said to be conspicuous. Such an external perception of India's self-reliance in AI arms build-up is significant. In my view, Delhi and Washington could optimise their AI collaboration, including in military terms, only after iCET and AD3 mature as deep partnerships.

An overarching objective of the UNGA's AI arms resolution was, arguably, responsible defence-related uses of AI. But, unlike India in November-December 2023, the US supported Austria's initiative in the UNGA to address challenges and concerns caused by the AI wave in the military domain.[26] Nonetheless, there was no US-India dissonance over the importance of the GGE process to consider the AI-LAWS issue in depth.

On balance, though, the nuanced mismatch between Delhi's and Washington's actual voting behaviour on that occasion is explainable. The US could protect and promote its numerous defence and strategic interests by exercising its vetoing right in the UNSC. In this ambient light, supporting a humanitarian cause in a non-binding UNGA resolution – which reflected international public opinion on the AI arms issue – was a tactical course for Washington.[27]

This was especially true at that time when America's image as a techno-democracy had suffered due to its enormous support for Israel in the latter's severe bombing campaign in Gaza. Israel, believed to possess AI-LAWS (besides the US, China and Russia), was already under considerable international scrutiny. Another tactical calculation that might have influenced the US became clear after it first voted for the AI arms resolution in the UNGA. Reciprocally, it seems, the member-states supported Washington's civil AI resolution in the UNGA on March 21, 2024 (elaborated further in Chapter 5).

On a separate aspect of voting on the AI arms resolution in the UNGA in November-December 2023, the Indian argument was, by and large, shared by China and Pakistan. This came as a surprise because Pakistan, unlike India, supported this AI arms resolution, while China abstained from voting. Japan voted for the resolution but expressed views similar to India's. However, India and Russia (despite the latter being close to Beijing as well in recent times) emerged as kindred souls by emphatically voting twice against this AI arms resolution.

Speaking after the voting in the UNGA's First Committee on November 1, 2023, China said the AI arms resolution "confuses lethal autonomous weapons with autonomous weapons". Sharing a strand of India's perspective on a pragmatic note, the Chinese representative said: "The Convention on Certain Conventional Weapons is the proper venue for discussing lethal autonomous weapons. Initiating a new discussion in the General Assembly would have a negative impact".[28] Participating 'constructively' in the relevant GGE process, China had also submitted, on December 13, 2021, a paper on "Regulating Military Applications of Artificial Intelligence".

Borderless AI Arms

In a relevant report published by the United Nations Institute for Disarmament Research (UNIDIR) in 2023, Sarah Grand-Clement classified the military applications of AI as upstream and downstream tasks. The deployment and use of AI-LAWS for the selection and engagement of targets would constitute downstream tasks.

All the prior tasks for producing and preparing these weapons for war would be upstream activities. The report noted that "ground-breaking revolutions in AI are not expected in the near future" until 2035 with respect to algorithms' upstream capabilities for data processing and reasoning.[29]

A summary of the UNIDIR report was alluded to by INDIAai, a portal jointly developed by India and a technology-trade association, on October

19, 2023. Therefore, India's arguable endorsement of the UNIDIR report and, separately, China's position paper of 2021 offered pointers to the respective attitudes of these two countries towards AI arms.

Focusing on the prior steps for using AI-LAWS, the Indian presentation discussed upstream tasks that are considered essential for the preparation and execution of any AI-powered military operation.[30] The upstream tasks would encompass command and control, information management, logistics and training – each step being related to the efficacy of AI-LAWS as weapons of choice. A major downstream task was identified as the need to address issues of meaningful human control, cybersecurity vulnerabilities and transparency. The purpose would be to ensure successful target selection and the desired application of AI exponential force.[31]

Two other challenges were identified – potential overreliance on AI-LAWS and the security as well as the integrity of black boxes in the event of these unmanned robots being downed. By thus drawing attention to the UNIDIR report, India appeared to focus on defending its own national security interest in the ambient light of borderless AI in global geopolitics. The Chinese position paper was, in contrast, a detailed checklist of steps for all countries, individually and collectively, to ensure global and regional strategic stability.[32] China sought to play the global mentor, keeping a watchful eye on the US as an existential rival. In a transparent salvo against the US in that position paper on AI, China emphasised the following message: "[All] countries need to bear in mind that military applications of AI shall never be used as a tool to start a war or pursue hegemony. We [the Chinese] oppose moves [by the US and/or its allies] to undermine the sovereignty and territorial security of other countries by using advantages in AI technology ".[33] The applicability of IHL and other relevant international laws, as well as when AI-LAWS were deployed and/or used in warfare, was also emphasised in the Chinese position paper. Another significant message was the need to ensure human control over and human responsibility for the deployment and use of AI-LAWS at all times. Because of AI's "dual-use nature", China called on all countries to work together to establish a universal regime and regulate all types of AI arms.[34]

Some Compatibility – Some Dissonance

These Chinese principles mostly sound rhetorical, but some may resonate as real propositions. In all, in outer space terminology, Beijing's assessment of AI-LAWS is not light-years away from India's, in strategic distance between the two countries.

Compatibility in the Sino-Indian views relates mainly to (1) human control over, and human responsibility for, AI arms; (2) the benchmarks of IHL and some relevant aspects of international law; and (3) the continuing relevance of discussions and/or negotiations within the Group of Governmental Experts' framework under the existing Convention on Certain Conventional Weapons.

India cannot easily associate itself with China's advocacy for each country's sovereignty as the absolute red line that should not be violated in any system of AI global governance. While cherishing the principle of national sovereignty, Delhi is also cognisant of AI's borderless expanse, which needs to be governed suitably. On another issue, Delhi is not directly involved in the Sino-American tussle over who is hegemonic and who desires to be hegemonic as the AI military superpower.

India has raised substantive but sensitive matters during the debates on AI in the UN chambers. This issue is one of providing a political bandwidth for using AI-powered lethal autonomous weapons in a war – "striking a balance between military necessity and humanitarian imperatives". China has not directly addressed this indispensable balance, while the US and India could discuss this in their dialogue on AI.

Within this spectrum of diplomacy to regulate the weaponisation of AI, Delhi re-published the UNIDIR's AI report, and Beijing submitted a position paper on military AI. These two documents served as the context for India's and China's explanations of their voting behaviour at the UNGA in November-December 2023. Surely unacceptable to India, though, is China's grandstanding as a global mentor on military AI. Surprisingly, the views of Pakistan and Japan on the AI arms resolution in the UNGA appeared to be in sync with the largely compatible attitudes of India and China. While India voted against, and China abstained from voting on, this AI arms resolution, Russia kept company with India. Japan and Pakistan cast positive votes. Japan and Pakistan endorsed the role of the Group of Governmental Experts (GGE), which was mandated to address military AI under the UN Convention on Certain Conventional Weapons (CCW).[35] Such support for the GGE under the UN's CCW was entirely in sync with India's position. With a number of other countries also being party to the UN's CCW, why was it necessary for the UNGA to adopt a specific resolution on AI-LAWS?

Evidently, protagonists of the UNGA's resolution on lethal autonomous weapons, especially AI-powered weapons, wanted to showcase international public opinion before the UN's September 2024 Summit of the Future.

Broad consensus on two key principles seems to have emerged from this public opinion exercise. These principles, with the least or no political and strategic opposition, are responsibility for, and human control over, the deployment and use of AI-LAWS in any conflict situation. In international relations, though, principles have a place only within a global, regional or even national calculus of power.

By and large, the empirical reality is that international relations are about competition and conflict and/or consensus and cooperation, depending on the assertiveness of state players at the centre stage. Non-state actors and/ or non-governmental organisations, as well as the civil society in various countries, may influence the actions of state players at the centre stage and outside it.

AI Arms: India-China, US-China Attitudes

The geopolitics of military AI, a grey zone in the inter-state relations of the 21st century's first quarter, may be determined by the countries vying for success as AI powers. Two pairs – India-China, as well as China-US – are among the few at the centre stage of this AI arms race. These countries may indeed stay their respective course into the future.

About the India-China rivalry, Prime Minister Modi (as already noted) had emphasised the role of AI for India's "strategic edge over the adversaries [China and Pakistan]". Also, as mentioned earlier, China is embedding AI-enabled "new types of combat forces" in its armoury (both these developments are referenced in Chapter 1).

Commenting on Beijing's moves, China specialist Ashok Kantha opinied that, "Artificial Intelligence will be deployed in China's defence architecture, as evident from [President] Xi Jinping's remarks during the National People's Congress [parliament] session in March 2024". According to Kantha, "AI will become an important tool in China's menu of military coercive actions against India and others".

In acute military terms, the AI tussle between China and the US is much more evident than the India-China AI equation, although the latter may sharpen. However, the attitudes of China and the US towards regulating the use of AI weapons matter not only to India but also to the entire international community. With Washington and Beijing commanding individual vetoing power in the UNSC, both view each other with deep suspicion about the future in the domain of military AI as well.

Beijing's thinly concealed hostility towards Washington, as noted earlier, is writ large in the Chinese 2021 paper on military AI and in China's Global AI Governance Initiative released in 2023. Washington's reciprocal wariness of Beijing is no secret, too. On July 13, 2021, US Defence Secretary Lloyd Austin minced no words against China's AI profile. Addressing a tech summit on AI, Austin said, "China's leaders have made clear they intend to be globally dominant in AI by the year 2030. Beijing has already talked about using AI for a range of missions, from surveillance to cyberattacks to autonomous weapons. In the AI realm, as in many others, we understand that China is our pacing challenge. We're going to compete to win, but we are going to do it the right way. We're not going to cut corners on safety, security, or ethics. And our watchwords are responsibility and results ".[36]

Relevant to this US-China contest (and the potential India-China equation) is the broad consensus at the UNGA about two indispensable principles: responsibility for using AI-LAWS under intelligent human control.

Notes

1. "Political Declaration on Responsible Military Use of Artificial Intelligence and Autonomy", *US Department of State*, https://www.state.gov/political-declaration-on-responsible-military-use-of-artificial-intelligence-and-autonomy-2/.
2. "The laws of war in a nutshell", *International Committee of the Red Cross*, https://www.icrc.org/en/document/what-are-rules-of-war-Geneva-Conventions.
3. "Secretary-General Urges Security Council to Ensure Transparency, Accountability, Oversight, in First Debate on Artificial Intelligence", *UN Press* ; https://press.un.org/en/2023/sgsm21880.doc.htm.
4. "What is IHL?", *International Committee of the Red Cross*, https://www.icrc.org/en/document/what-ihl.
5. This author's interpretation of the applicability of Geneva Conventions in the rapidly evolving AI age.
6. Jean-Marc Rickli and Federico Mantellassi, "Artificial Intelligence in Warfare: Military Uses of AI and Their International Security Implications", *The AI Wave in Defence Innovation: Assessing Military Artificial Intelligence Strategies, Capabilities, and Trajectories*, Edited by Michael Raska and Richard A. Bitzinger (Oxon and New York: Routledge, 2023), pp. 23—24.
7. Ibid, p.23.

8. "First Committee Approves New Resolution on Lethal Autonomous Weapons, as Speaker Warns 'An Algorithm Must Not Be in Full Control of Decisions Involving Killing'", *UN Press*, https://press.un.org/en/2023/gadis3731.doc.htm#:~:text=Even%20if%20an%20algorithm%20can,56 (Last accessed on February 29, 2024). For the resolution text, see: United Nations, A/C.1/78/L.56.
9. Ibid.
10. Ibid.
11. "UN First Committee : India's Explanation of Vote (POST-VOTING): Conventional Weapons Cluster, 78th UNGA First Committee, UNHQ, New York, October 2023," *Permanent Mission of India to the Conference on Disarmament*, Geneva, https://meaindia.nic.in/cdgeneva/?18348?000.
12. "Statement By Ambassador Anupam Ray At The Group Of Governmental Experts On Emerging Technologies In The Area Of Lethal Autonomous Weapons Systems– Geneva, March 6, 2023", *Permanent Mission of India to the Conference on Disarmament*, Geneva, https://meaindia.nic.in/cdgeneva/?17714?000.
13. n.11.
14. n.11.
15. "Convention on Certain Conventional Weapons : Interventions by Ambassador Pankaj Sharma, Permanent Representative of India to the Conference on Disarmament during the First Session of the 2021 GGE on LAWS (August 3-13, 2021)" *Permanent Mission of India to the Conference on Disarmament*, Geneva, ; https://meaindia.nic.in/cdgeneva/?13789?000.
16. Ibid.
17. Based on India's call for a *balance* between military and humanitarian objectives, this author has interpreted the nuances in Delhi's calculus on AI-LAWS. China's "Global AI Governance Initiative", unveiled at the BRF session in October 2023, governs that country's updated position on AI-LAWS as well.
18. "General Assembly Adopts $3.59 Billion Budget for 2024, Establishes Funding for Peacebuilding, Concluding Main Part of Seventy-eighth Session" *UN Press*, https://press.un.org/en/2023/ga12578.doc.htm.
19. Yasushi Kaneko, "U.N. General Assembly Calls for Rulemaking on 'Killer AI'; Russia, India Cast Only 'No' Votes; China, Israel Abstain", *The Japan News*,https://japannews.yomiuri.co.jp/politics/defense-security/20231223-157527/.
20. Ibid.
21. "English rendering of PM's address at the inauguration of GPAI Summit, 2023", *Prime Minister's Office*, https://pib.gov.in/PressReleasePage.aspx?PRID=1985614.
22. These two India-US technology initiatives are referenced in Chapter 3.
23. "Readout of the Inaugural U.S. – India Advanced Domains Defense Dialogue", *U.S. Department of Defense*,; https://www.defense.gov/News/Releases/Release/

Article/3408336/readout-of-the-inaugural-us-india-advanced-domains-defense-dialogue/.

24. Ibid.
25. Antoine Levesques, “Early steps in India's use of AI for defence”, *IISS*, https://www.iiss.org/online-analysis/online-analysis/2024/01/early-steps-in-indias-use-of-ai-for-defence/.
26. n.8.
27. This author's interpretation based on the transforming international geostrategic cross-currents at the beginning of 2024.
28. n.8.
29. Sarah Grand-Clement, “Artificial Intelligence Beyond Weapons Application and Impact of AI in the Military Domain”, *UNIDIR*,https://unidir.org/wp-content/uploads/2023/10/UNIDIR_AI_Beyond_Weapons_Application_Impact_AI_in_the_Military_Domain.pdf.
30. “Artificial Intelligence Beyond Weapons: Application and Impact of AI in the Military Domain”, *INDIAai*, https://indiaai.gov.in/research-reports/artificial-intelligence-beyond-weapons-application-and-impact-of-ai-in-the-military-domain.
31. Ibid.
32. “Position Paper of the People's Republic of China on Regulating Military Applications of Artificial Intelligence (AI)”, *China's Permanent Mission to the United Nations Office at Geneva*, http://geneva.china-mission.gov.cn/eng/dbdt/202112/t20211213_10467517.htm#:~:text=In%20terms%20of%20strategic%20security,undermining%20of%20strategic%20mutual%20trust%2C.
33. Ibid.
34. Ibid.
35. n.8.
36. “Secretary of Defense Austin Remarks at the Global Emerging Technology Summit of The National Security Commission on Artificial Intelligence (As Delivered)”, US Department of Defence, https://www.defense.gov/News/Transcripts/Transcript/Article/2692943/secretary-of-defense-austin-remarks-at-the-global-emerging-technology-summit-of/.

5

US-China Tussle to Ride The Cascading AI Wave

Time and tide waits for none. This ancient adage was about the speed of time and the power of cascading tide. These two aspects apply to the expanding global challenges of governing post-modern artificial intelligence (AI). In 2023, the United Nations (UN) began recognising AI as a cascading tidal wave of hyper-advanced technology. Its civil and military applications were reckoned to be formidable, necessitating a suitable response from the international community. A high-level advisory body on artificial intelligence was launched by the UN.[1]

The UN was already exploring global governance of the cyber-digital realm. In that ambience, the recognition of AI was, by far, an easy step ahead of the UN's September 2024 Summit of the Future. Ironically, with AI progressing at almost the speed of light, the future telescopes into the present at any given time. Almost every UN member-state wanted to look like a good global citizen and was, therefore, agreeable to recognising AI as almost humanity's new destiny. Gradually, however, geopolitical bloc-thinking by different interest groups led or inspired by the United States (US) and China, respectively, became evident, too.

AI is not the monopoly of any state or non-state actor. However, the US and China have begun to act as if they hold the trump card to lead. In this writing, the European Union and India are prominent among the other players to watch. But the US-China rivalry hogs the headlines.

Stealing a march over China, the US pulled off a diplomatic triumph at the UN General Assembly (UNGA) on March 21, 2024. The Assembly unanimously adopted a US-led draft resolution[2] on regulating AI in all its applications for sustainable development (hereinafter, 'Civil AI Resolution', to distinguish it from the UNGA's AI arms resolution). The UNGA's first AI resolution was adopted in December 2023 and focused entirely on AI-powered Lethal Autonomous Weapons Systems (AI-LAWS).[3] India voted against that resolution on AI arms (as exemplified by the AI-LAWS) for reasons already discussed.[4] Significantly, India was, by and large, privy to the US-led initiative that culminated in the UNGA's Civil AI Resolution. When the UNGA put out the draft dated March 11, 2024, India, along with China, did not figure in the list of co-sponsors of this resolution. On March 14, however, Washington disclosed a list of 54 co-sponsors, including India,[5] for the same draft of the resolution. China did not appear on that list again. A joint statement by the US and these co-sponsors, including India, was issued, advocating for the Civil AI Resolution. This could mean that India supported the US initiative after carefully studying the nuances. Finally, by March 21, more than 120 member-states, including China,[6] co-sponsored the US-led resolution, facilitating global consensus on regulating AI for worldwide economic and social development.

US Characteristics in UNGA's View on Civil AI

The promotion of safe, secure and trustworthy artificial intelligence[7] is the centrepiece of this document. Another highlight is the respect for human rights in the design, development, deployment and use of AI. Protection and promotion of human rights are also mandated. Recognised, too, in this Civil AI Resolution is the potential of AI systems to enable and accelerate progress towards the attainment of the UN's Sustainable Development Goals.[8]

Claiming credit for this resolution, US National Security Advisor Jake Sullivan said "a baseline set of principles" would guide AI's development and use.[9] To gain universal consensus over this comprehensive resolution, the US spent countless hours of negotiations with other UN member-states over a period of almost four months.

As a result, the crowning glory, in Sullivan's view, was this: "Critically, the resolution makes clear that protecting human rights and fundamental freedoms must be central to the development and use of AI systems".[10]

Categorical, too, in the resolution is the affirmation of the supremacy of international law for regulating AI for worldwide economic and social development.[11] It is also clarified in the text that the resolution deals with only the non-military AI advancement and use for attaining the UN's sustainable development goals.

Two significant points were made by US Permanent Representative to the UN, Thomas-Greenfield after the resolution was adopted. She called for collective commitment to "closing the digital gap within and between nations". For the international community, in her view, a new opportunity, laced with responsibility, was "to govern this technology rather than let it govern us".[12]

Delhi, as a member of the Quad, did not have any consensus-busting difference with Washington over the Civil AI Resolution. Moreover, India shared (and continues to share) America's overarching view of the opportunities and concerns about AI. Both countries are also engaged in exploring these aspects through the Indo-US Initiative on Critical and Emerging Technologies (iCET) and Advanced Domains Defence Dialogue (AD3). Technological parameters of this bilateral collaboration, arising out of the iCET and AD3, are outside the scope of this book on diplomacy. By accepting the US-led AI resolution, what did China, a late co-sponsor, seek to convey, especially after having floated its own Global AI Governance Initiative with Chinese characteristics?

In the absence of a formal Chinese comment, state-linked Global Times said the UNGA's Civil AI Resolution was a joint proposal by the US and co-sponsors, including China. By co-signing the draft, China demonstrated its responsible attitude towards the global governance of AI. It was further claimed that China's commitment to true multilateralism was evident from this episode.[13] All this appeared to be just a Chinese gloss-over, allowing the US to take the lead on this important issue.

'US-Led' AI Globalism versus 'Chinese' Globalism

Two major geopolitical issues – Israel's relentless war against Hamas in Gaza and the cascading AI tidal wave – were in prime focus at the UN in March 2024. Of these two, the raging war was widely seen as the primary concern of the Security Council, while AI had not yet come up for a vote there. China, the aspiring Asian and global hegemon, despite its disavowals in this regard, was clearly engaged in challenging the US over its long-standing global leadership.

Exemplifying the constant Chinese caricature of America in recent times, China's state media wrote on March 25 that the so-called US 'world leadership' is deep in the red. The choice of the word red, denoting a colour associated with China, seemed like its Freudian slip for aspiration to unseat the US from its pedestal or share that position. Furthermore, China's state news agency demanded that Washington abandon its obsession with being the indispensable leader of the world. Indeed, Washington should "behave first like a responsible player".[14]

The commentary appeared after Washington successfully piloted the Civil AI Resolution in the UNGA and after China vetoed a US resolution in the UNSC on the Gaza crisis. In that ambience, Washington proved its diplomatic skill to lead on the AI issue, while China checkmated the US on the diplomatic chessboard over a humanitarian crisis in Gaza. These outcomes do not reflect a fractured reality of the US and China carving out respective areas of influence. Instead, both seek leadership roles in all domains, including AI.

AI is widely seen as the domain that could determine the global pecking order of powerful and influential countries. Unsurprisingly, on March 7, China spelt out its ambition to play a big role at the UN in the context of the September 2024 Summit of the Future. Before Washington got the Civil AI Resolution adopted at the UNGA, Chinese Foreign Minister Wang Yi spoke of submitting to the same Assembly a draft on AI-related international cooperation. The Chinese draft would be focused on "enhancing international cooperation on capacity-building of artificial intelligence", Wang Yi said. Such cooperation would be sought by encouraging technology sharing to "bridge the AI divide" among the UN member-states. Calling for an "equal emphasis on [economic] development and [international] security" in the global administration of AI, Wang Yi suggested three principles for harnessing the hyper-technology's explosive growth.[15] China would seek to ensure that "AI is a force for good" for all humanity, besides being safe and fair.

First, as a force for good', the development of AI should be ethical and in conformity with international law as well as the undefined current trend of human civilisation. Second, perpetual human control would be required to ensure safety. This would necessitate "plans to assess and control various kinds of risks" in improving the development of AI on interpretable and predictable lines. Third, the principle of fairness could be pursued, with the UN setting up "an international AI governance institution" – all member-states being entitled to equal terms of participation and benefits.[16]

Wang Yi proposed these apparently actionable steps to implement China's Global AI Governance Initiative,[17] unveiled in October 2023 as an output of Xi Jinping Thought on Diplomacy. As Xi's strategic salvo at global mentoring, as noted earlier, the initiative was replete with exhortations of 'dos and don'ts' for the AI players, especially sovereign states. Therefore, Wang Yi's invocation of the interests of all humanity was (and still is) a mantra that could resonate among many sections of the UN.

The Heartbeat of Algorithm

To capture the minds and hearts of the UN, Beijing has to compete with Washington, especially after the latter generated a global consensus on civil AI on March 21, 2024. What, therefore, were (and, indeed, are) the key ideological and geopolitical AI narratives orchestrated respectively by the US and China?

US Secretary of State Antony Blinken, addressing the Third Summit for Democracy in Seoul on March 17, noted the worldwide optimism about the potential for AI. Democracies, he said, "are positioned to harness that optimism, but AI is also a critical arena in which democracy is being challenged".[18] Above all, Blinken said, "the United States is determined to shape the terms of our technological future" in all arenas, including AI. He characterised such a future as a dispensation "that's inclusive, rights-respecting, that sustains democratic values and democratic institutions". The US had already invested in its own technological capabilities and in those of its democratic partners. Blinken's punchline was that Washington had begun "pairing those investments with efforts to lead on the governance of artificial intelligence".[19]

Blinken's statements marked a candid public disclosure of America's global AI leadership ambitions and agenda. Unsurprisingly, China, seeing itself as the ideological opponent of US-style democracy, lost little time to question US leadership of democracies in any arena, including AI. Reacting to Blinken's remarks, a Chinese spokesperson said, "China always (sic) opposes drawing lines on ideological grounds and using democracy-related issues as [strategic] tools or weapons".[20]

Although Blinken identified democracy as the heartbeat of AI algorithms in all but name, Sullivan's remarks and a close scrutiny of the Civil AI Resolution reveal a nuanced reality. Sullivan summed up this resolution as "a baseline set of principles" to guide civil AI's development and use.[21]

Furthermore, the Civil AI Resolution remains singularly bereft of democracy as the political and/or strategic inspiration for the development and use of this hyper-advanced technology. The reason is not far to seek. Washington had to settle for the least common denominators in terms of principles so that a global consensus could be secured. However, the consensus resolution was (and is) at best cold comfort for Beijing.

Some salient principles enshrined in this resolution, despite its non-binding character, were not advocated by China in its Global AI Governance Initiative. China's most cherished value in administering AI as well – the inviolability of national sovereignty[22] – was conspicuously ignored as a foundational principle in the US-piloted Civil AI Resolution.[23] China accepted the resolution but did not (or could not) persuade the US to accept the AI principle of national sovereignty – during the confidential negotiations among the UN member-states.

India, too, values national sovereignty very dearly while also recognising AI's global canvas that extends to Outer Space (briefly highlighted in Chapter 4). However, even in this AI age, Delhi resists any perceived attempt by the US to interfere, by word or deed, in India's sovereign affairs.

Mincing no words, on March 27, 2024, while criticising a comment by the US State Department on India's legal system, the External Affairs Ministry said: "In diplomacy, states are expected to be respectful of the sovereignty and internal affairs of others. This responsibility is even more so in [the] case of fellow democracies [like India and the US]".[24]

The categorical reference to "sovereignty and internal affairs" of "fellow democracies" indicates that India might zealously guard its AI-related internal matters of sovereignty. On regional and global dimensions of AI, though, Delhi might be willing to actively collaborate with the US. Such a logical inference based on India's red line on national sovereignty is not identical to China's campaign for state sovereignty in the internal and global areas of AI. However, India knows, like China, that drawing a clear line between national sovereignty and global good on the AI turf is a big challenge.

In effect, Delhi seems aware that the heartbeat of algorithms is induced by the advancements of technology rather than geopolitics or ethics. The US-India Strategic Technology Partnership (without a military dimension, at this writing) – besides Delhi's participation in the AI-related forums like GPAI, Bletchley conference on safe 'Frontier AI', etc. – reveals this geostrategic factor.

A Battle over Geopolitical Values

Other key Chinese principles not incorporated in the US-piloted UNGA resolution were emblematic of Beijing's opposition to the perceived US bid for global AI leadership. The list centres on opposition to unilateral coercive measures through technological monopolies, intervention in other countries' internal affairs, pro-democracy ideological lines, disinformation, and disruption of the global AI supply chain. Washington assiduously avoided glorifying any aspect of Chinese objections as a norm of global governance in the UNGA's Civil AI Resolution.

The liberal US values incorporated in this resolution were accepted by China because it could interpret them to suit its authoritarian worldview instead of relying on America's textbook norms. "Human rights and fundamental freedoms must be respected, protected and promoted throughout the life cycle of artificial intelligence systems" it was emphasised in the resolution. The life cycle of civil AI systems, as outlined in the document, covers pre-design, design, development, evaluation, testing, deployment, use, sale, procurement, operation and decommissioning – each process being human-centric.

Whether the US, not just China, and their respective AI agencies and technologists would always observe the human-centric dictum could prove to be an endless argument. Surely, China is widely believed to practise ubiquitous state control over the entire spectrum of AI processes. But the same cannot be said of the US. This would only complicate the monitoring of state- and non-state behaviour, especially in the absence of an agreed international mechanism for verification to ensure compliance. So, a non-partisan argument runs in this writing.

A counter-argument is that the resolution is only a first step in conceptualising principles, which could be converted into actionable step(s) sooner or later. Hope and time will tell if this counter-argument will be fulfilled. However, the non-binding nature of this resolution made it acceptable to all UN member-states which have no uniform system of either internal governance or external policy. If this is considered to be a cynical view, an alternative is to see this Civil AI Resolution as a reflection of idealistic international public opinion. A formidable reality and sensitivity check, though, is the credibility of each UN member state's commitment to promote "safe, reliable and trustworthy AI" for both national and global good. In particular, the US and China will be watching each other closely. The dictum of 'trust but verify' may itself be a tall order both ways in this US-China relationship. This, in turn, will have implications for other countries, especially India, in the futurist AI domain.

Other US-favoured principles that permeated the resolution included national "obligations under international law" and "protection of personal data" and the UN's centrality, with representation for developing countries, in AI governance. For the reasons discussed, these principles, too, received universal support, including from India and China.

US-China AI Race and Beyond

Despite the Sino-American wariness towards each other, Brookings' commentary has advocated for cooperation between Washington and Beijing. "China is first out of the box with a regulatory structure for AI, including for the new generative AI services .... Engagement with China's regulators and experts on their experience [in] developing and implementing AI law and policy would be in the best interests of Western regulators".[25]

Drawing a distinction between US-led digital democracy and Chinese digital authoritarianism, the commentary underscores as follows: "Of course, China's rigid ideological control of public discourse is based on a level of government surveillance, censorship, and propaganda that is simply unacceptable in liberal democracies. This ideological control [in China] is in full view in the new [Chinese] AI rules .... With eyes wide open to these risks, it would be overwhelmingly important for Western policymakers to see what can be learned from China's experience [in] regulating AI. China is open to learning from [AI] developments abroad".[26]

US policy leaders and opinion makers see risks in the Sino-American AI equation beyond the distinction between the ideologies of digital democracy and digital authoritarianism. Defence-related AI, too, figures in this equation. Calls for AI arms control[27] show that there is more to the US-China AI race than meets the eye as a technological issue in global governance. It is said that "America and China must work together to avert catastrophe".[28]

However, as we saw in Chapter 4, the US voted for the AI arms resolution in the UNGA in December 2023, while China abstained from voting. China cited some reasons similar to those of India, which voted against that resolution on AI-powered lethal autonomous weapons systems (AI-LAWS). While this aspect might be a fleeting episode in the US-China rivalry, the geopolitics of their AI arms control cannot be ignored in global governance for long.

As a rising AI power, India deserves a place in a future control room for global governance of the emerging AI race among more than one pair of countries. Henry Kissinger focused attention only on the perceived pair of AI superpowers[29] – the US and China. However, they are not the only countries with substantial AI capabilities and aspirations. As Russian President Vladimir Putin is reported to have remarked, "Whoever becomes the leader in this sphere [of artificial intelligence] will become the ruler of the world".[30]

Notes

1. António Guterres, "Secretary-General's remarks at press conference launching High-Level Advisory Body on Artificial Intelligence", *United Nations*, https://www.un.org/sg/en/content/sg/speeches/2023-10-26/secretary-general%E2%80%99s-remarks-press-conference-launching-high-level-advisory-body-artificial-intelligence%C2%A0.
2. "United Nations General Assembly Adopts by Consensus U.S.-Led Resolution on Seizing the Opportunities of Safe, Secure and Trustworthy Artificial Intelligence Systems for Sustainable Development", *US Department of State*, https://www.state.gov/united-nations-general-assembly-adopts-by-consensus-u-s-led-resolution-on-seizing-the-opportunities-of-safe-secure-and-trustworthy-artificial-intelligence-systems-for-sustainable-development/.
3. See Chapter 4 for the geopolitics of AI arms resolution at the UNGA.
4. Ibid.
5. "Joint Statement on the Proposed UNGA Resolution on Seizing the Opportunities of Safe, Secure, and Trustworthy AI Systems for Sustainable Development", *US Mission to the UN*, ; https://usun.usmission.gov/joint-statement-on-the-proposed-unga-resolution-on-seizing-the-opportunities-of-safe-secure-and-trustworthy-ai-systems-for-sustainable-development/.
6. Liu Xin and Li Meng, "Cooperation among major countries important to AI devt as UNGA adopts landmark AI resolution: expert", *Global Times*, https://

www.globaltimes.cn/page/202403/1309345.shtml#:~:text=The%20United%20 Nations%20General%20Assembly,participating%20in%20the%20joint%20proposal (Last accessed on March 23, 2024).

7. "General Assembly adopts landmark resolution on artificial intelligence", *UN News*, https://news.un.org/en/story/2024/03/1147831
8. Ibid.
9. "Statement from National Security Advisor Jake Sullivan on the United Nations General Assembly Resolution on Artificial Intelligence for Sustainable Development", *The White House*, https://www.whitehouse.gov/briefing-room/statements-releases/2024/03/21/statement-from-national-security-advisor-jake-sullivan-on-the-united-nations-general-assembly-resolution-on-artificial-intelligence-for-sustainable-development/.
10. Ibid.
11. For the text of UNGA's civil AI resolution, see: https://undocs.org/a/78/l.49.
12. n.7.
13. n.6.
14. "U.S. "world leadership" in the red - China Military", *China Military*, http://eng.chinamil.com.cn/OPINIONS_209196/Opinions_209197/16296600.html.
15. "Member of the Political Bureau of the CPC Central Committee and Foreign Minister Wang Yi Meets the Press", *Ministry of Foreign Affairs*, PRC, https://www.fmprc.gov.cn/eng/zxxx_662805/202403/t20240307_11255682.html.
16. Ibid.
17. Xi Jinping's "AI Global Governance Initiative" is referenced and discussed in Chapter 3.
18. "Secretary Antony J. Blinken At the Ministerial Conference of the Third Summit for Democracy", *US Embassy in China*, https://china.usembassy-china.org.cn/secretary-antony-j-blinken-at-the-ministerial-conference-of-the-third-summit-for-democracy/.
19. Ibid.
20. "Foreign Ministry Spokesperson Lin Jian's Regular Press Conference on March 18, 2024", *Ministry of Foreign Affairs*, PRC, https://www.fmprc.gov.cn/eng/xwfw_665399/s2510_665401/2511_665403/202403/t20240318_11262102.html.
21. n.9.
22. "Global AI Governance Initiative--The Third Belt and Road Forum for International Cooperation", Belt and Road Forum, (referenced in Chapter 3).
23. n.7.
24. "India strongly objects to the remarks of the US State Department Spokesperson", *Ministry of External Affairs*, GoI, https://www.mea.gov.in/press-releases.htm?dtl/37748/India_strongly_objects_to_the_remarks_of_the_US_State_Department_Spokesperson.

25. Mark MacCarthy, "The US and its allies should engage with China on AI law and policy", *Brookings* Commentary, https://www.brookings.edu/articles/the-us-and-its-allies-should-engage-with-china-on-ai-law-and-policy/#:~:text=In%20March%202022%2C%20it%20promulgated,video%2C%20audio%2C%20and%20text.
26. Ibid.
27. Henry A. Kissinger and Graham Allison, Article in *Foreign Affairs* (October 13, 2023), The Path to AI Arms Control, https://www.foreignaffairs.com/united-states/henry-kissinger-path-artificial-intelligence-arms-control.
28. Ibid.
29. Ibid.
30. "Raksha Mantri launches 75 Artificial Intelligence products/technologies during first-ever 'AI in Defence' symposium & exhibition in New Delhi; Terms AI as a revolutionary step in the development of humanity", *Ministry of Defence*, https://pib.gov.in/PressReleasePage.aspx?PRID=1840740.

6

Cyber-Digital Domains: High-Tech Core of the Times

Cyberspace and the digital domain are most commonly accessed through computers and mobile phones. They are powered by various types and characteristics of hyper-advanced technology. Often treated as being interlinked, both these domains breathe in and breathe out electronic data. The key difference, though, cyberspace is entirely a non-physical field; digital devices used to access cyberspace have physical attributes. Software and software-compatible hardware are required to access the cyberspace. Chips, which require semiconductors, make the digital products work. Security concerns about the use of both these extensively-accessed grey zones have proliferated. A fair system of global, regional, or country-specific governance is, therefore, the need of the hour. However, a key puzzle is who will govern and how.

A notable early attempt in this regard was the drafting of the Tallinn Manual. Known at first as the Tallinn Manual on the International Law Applicable to Cyber Warfare, the non-enforceable scholarly compilation[1] was achieved by 2013. This exercise was undertaken at the behest of the Tallinn (Estonia)-based 'NATO Cooperative Cyber Defence Centre of Excellence'.[2]

An international cyberspace treaty has been a goalpost that those engaged in drafting the Tallinn Manual have kept in mind. Ahead of the

September 2024 UN Summit of the Future, the outlook for such a treaty, essentially in regard to cybersecurity, did not look very bright.

Perceived as an increasingly global 'military' organisation controlled by the US, the NATO Centre is viewed with scepticism, even hostility, by China out of its competitive urge and concerns. Although outside of NATO, Japan has now joined this Centre,[3] raising China's anxieties further.

Beijing is also concerned about the 'Five Eyes', an intelligence-sharing alliance among the US, the United Kingdom, Canada, Australia and New Zealand. The 'Five Eyes Intelligence Oversight and Review Council' says that its members engage among themselves and with other countries as, when and where appropriate.[4] The principle of appropriateness means that such engagements would inevitably take place within the bounds of secrecy and transparency as the parties concerned wish to maintain. Moreover, the apparent mandate of the 'Five Eyes' is not restricted to a close watch over the cyberspace operations of key countries. In criticising this alliance, though, China seems deeply concerned about the apparent permissiveness in global cyberspace.

India knows that China is not the only country that feels like it is being 'watched' by the 'Five Eyes'. India and China, too, have their respective cybersecurity organisations. In addition, the US is deepening its cyberspace cooperation with India. On the digital side, the production of upscale iPhones began in India in 2022, during a partial shift from China, and as a mark of strategic trust in India.

Cyber Sovereignty

As a 'global mentor' in this overall context, China issued a white paper in November 2022 under the title of 'Jointly Build a Community with a Shared Future in Cyberspace'.[5] Propagating a slogan of the undefined shared future, Beijing points out that a relevant UNGA resolution on information security enshrines this Chinese mantra. 'Respect for the cyber sovereignty of all countries' is the crux of this white paper.

Striking a dissonant note vis-à-vis the West, China expressed its respect for the independent right of every country to choose its own model of network management. Every state should be allowed to pursue its own public policy on internet issues. In this respect, all countries should enjoy the "right to equal participation in international cyberspace governance".[6] In a punchline, Beijing advocated that "a just and rational" international cyberspace order be "built on the basis of national sovereignty".[7] Subsumed in this formula is the Chinese insistence that ordinary citizens, corporate players and other legitimate non-state actors – widely recognised as stakeholders – must follow the relevant state's ideological line.

Unanswered in the Chinese white paper is a puzzle. If Beijing wants its ideological purity to be maintained, what indeed is the scope for China to share its future with countries that have other national ideologies or priorities? Just as master and servant could share their future without losing their current imbalanced equation, does China want countries with asymmetric power quotients to remain asymmetric in a shared future? If so, a shared future will not bring equal or equivalent benefits to all countries. They would be sharing the future with just the passage of time.

In July 2022, China floated its own global platform known as the 'World Internet Conference'. China is not the only country wanting to have 'soul mates' in these grey zones. More specifically, on May 25, 2023, China outlined its 'Positions on Global Digital Governance', thereby seeking to promote the UN's Global Digital Compact. Primarily, Beijing demands that the sovereignty of any state over the data gathered within its territorial jurisdiction should be respected. While this is not a lonely voice, Beijing seeks to leverage its status in the UN Security Council to shape and sustain a China-friendly global compact.

India's Pragmatic 'Priorities'

Delhi, for its part, appears to seek an 'internationalistic' solution in a pragmatic fashion. Before the September 2024 UN Summit of the Future, the priorities India outlined for itself revealed the approach of a globalist with no unilateral guidelines for all countries (discussed in Chapter 3). This crucial aspect distinguishes India from China in the latter's sermon-like globalism. Delhi adopted a softer, not strident, line even on the points compatible with Beijing's. Some salient aspects of India's priorities were an inclusive digital ecosystem covering all countries, a digital future for all as might be agreed, technology transfer as needed, and UN reforms.[8]

Separately, India and the European Union (EU) established a working group on 'Strategic Technologies, Digital Governance and Digital Connectivity'. The group held its first ministerial meeting in Brussels in May 2023.

In May 2018, the EU began implementing its General Data Protection Regulation (GDPR), said to be the world's "toughest privacy and security law".[9] It applies to any organisation targeting and/or collecting data relating to people resident in Europe. With the EU seeking to set a gold standard in cyber-digital domains, India faces opportunities and challenges in this bilateral working group on strategic technologies.

India and the US hold compatible views on the technological importance of the cyber-digital domains for the future of life and work in the world. On April 11, 2022, US Defence Secretary Lloyd Austin noted that his country was deepening its cooperation with India in the cyberspace. This encompassed cyberspace-related training and exercises planned for later that year. More emphatically, he said the US and India "are expanding our information-sharing partnership across all warfighting domains".[10] These included the cyberspace. Yet, despite being the world's two largest democracies, India and the US do differ in some perspectives about these high-tech domains.

Significantly, India did not sign the US-piloted 'Declaration for the Future of the Internet' on April 29, 2022.[11] This happened within days after Austin had spoken about the deepening US-India cooperation in cyberspace. Ups and downs in inter-state cooperation, based on the perceived national interests of the partners at any given time, are not uncommon. On March 27, 2024, India told the US that it should not cast unwarranted aspersions on India's legal processes.

Delhi does not really favour digital authoritarianism, which the US-drafted Declaration for the Future of the Internet opposes. Nonetheless, Delhi might wish to explore the idea of a 'single global Internet', as embedded in the US-led Declaration, with much pragmatism. China's sermon-like unilateral agenda of digital protectionism is for the entire world, except the US. From India's perspective, China's digital protectionism and America's campaign for a universal internet may require a reality check in a truly diverse world.

Cybersecurity on the Global Agenda

Cyberspace is at the heart or core of the ecosystem of hyper-advanced technologies that include AI. Without cyberspace, the operability of other high-tech domains is almost impossible to imagine. Unsurprising, therefore, is that cybersecurity has become a major concern that the UN Security Council has begun to address.

The UNSC held its first-ever debate on cyber threats, which need to be countered to ensure cybersecurity, on June 29, 2021. The UNGA had previously set up two panels under the rubric of international security. These are (1) the Group of Governmental Experts to promote "responsible state behaviour in cyberspace and (2) the Open-Ended Working Group on Information and Communications Technology (ICT). UN's High Representative for Disarmament Affairs Izumi Nakamitsu identified the main cyber threats as those targeting the ICT-reliant infrastructure such as energy grids, financial institutions and health-care facilities. She commended the work of the UNGA-established groups in addressing the proliferating cyber threats.[12]

The views voiced by representatives of some key cyberspace-savvy states reveal nuances of how this core domain should be governed. Kaja Kallas, Prime Minister of Estonia (UNSC President for that month), emphasised the applicability of existing international law to activities of both states and non-state actors in cyberspace. She also called on the corporate sector to invest in institutions and activities relevant to cybersecurity. The US called for the protection of internet freedom while ensuring cybersecurity.[13] Critics of the US see internet freedom as a permissive cyberspace.

India urged the adoption of a rules-based approach in cyberspace.[14] The rules-based international order (RBO) is often associated with the US (as the architect of this concept). India's call for a rules-based approach was not necessarily the same as RBO, which, in the eyes of the critics of the US, would be a selective application of international law.

The prevention of an arms race in cyberspace and a warning against technological hegemony were among the points made by the Chinese representative during the UNSC debate.[15] Cyber sovereignty of all nations, encompassing their right to develop their respective internet, was China's other key point of advocacy. In yet another code for criticism of the US, the Chinese representative said cyberspace should not be a new battlefield.

Truly, China had initiated a cyber war of words against the US, with the latter not fighting shy of such a war. Indeed, from a Chinese perspective, the US had fired the 'first shot' in this 'war of words', with a real cyber war, too, looming if not prevented.

Tiny Chips with Gigantic Impact

The centrality of semiconductors (also known as integrated circuits and, most popularly, chips) for hyper-advanced technologies is well-recognised. It has been a continually game-changing story from the US-Soviet tussle for Cold War Chips to China's rise as a high-tech power posing a challenge to American tech supremacy.[16]

Chinese President Xi Jinping has sought to emerge, in positive terms, as a tech-savvy post-modern 'Maoist'. Author Chris Miller has narrated how Xi's agenda "was about remaking the world's semiconductor industry, not integrating with it".[17]

Elsewhere, the US launched the 'Chip 4 Alliance' in February 2023, drawing a furious reaction from China. (The US, Taiwan, Japan and South Korea constitute the 'Chip 4 Alliance'). There is scepticism, too, in some quarters about how far the 'Chip 4 Alliance' can go in the face of China's resolute opposition.

On a parallel track, Washington began efforts to block the transfer of US-origin high-tech chips to China. Some of America's allies and partners followed suit. This particular American strategy was intensified in the light of a relevant executive order signed by President Joe Biden in August 2023. He declared a national emergency[18] to deal with the technology threat from countries of concern like China. About a year earlier, the US had enacted the 'CHIPS and Science Act' in August 2022 to counter China[19], besides trying to boost the American economy.

Although not the same as the 'Chip 4 alliance', the Quad consistently focuses its attention on cybersecurity and digital issues. Cybersecurity has been a key concern at the Quad Summit since its inauguration in 2021. At the Quad leaders' Tokyo summit in May 2022, 'Joint Principles for Cybersecurity Partnership' was spelt out. Going forward, at the Hiroshima summit on May 20, 2023, the Quad announced 'Joint Principles for Secure Software'. Also outlined were 'Principles for Cybersecurity of Critical Infrastructure'.

Such cross-currents in the attempts by major powers to administer these twin grey zones show the challenge. An issue is whether these cross-currents could merge. An alternative is to manage these cross-currents through an agreed mechanism.

Critical and Emerging Technologies

Broadly, critical and emerging technologies are those considered essential for the national security and defence of any state in the strategic, political, economic, public health and societal domains. The range of such know-how is vast – from semiconductors with varied civil and military applications to deterrence-evading hypersonic glide missiles.

China's emergence as a key player in the 5G telecom sector served as a wake-up call for the US-led West and India about the Chinese prowess in critical technologies. Furthermore, the negative impact of China's expanding control of the industrial and other supply chains, some of which were deemed critical, was felt internationally during the COVID-19 pandemic in the early part of the 2020s.

Cumulatively, the urgency of safeguarding national security in the domains of critical and emerging technologies cannot be over-emphasised. The Quad seems to be leading the way in addressing this issue in the absence of a concerted global initiative. However, China, with its windfall vetoing right in the UN Security Council since 1971, poses a serious challenge to the Quad's efforts at addressing many issues concerning critical technologies. It has begun to formulate principles and standardise norms for the design and dissemination of critical technologies. The formation of a 'Critical and Emerging Technology Working Group' was decided when the Quad leaders held a video-linked summit in March 2021. At the first-ever in-person Quad summit in Washington in September 2021, it was announced that contact groups, one each on AI and Advanced Communications, would be set up. The leaders also decided to launch a 'Semiconductor Supply Chain Initiative'.[20] At the second in-person Quad summit in Tokyo in May 2022, 'Principles for Critical Technology Supply Chain Security' was formulated.

A 'Statement on International Standards Cooperation Network' and 'Principles on Critical and Emerging Technology Standards'[21] were released at the Quad summit in Hiroshima on May 20, 2023. Overarching the several documents of that summit, the Quad leaders issued a Vision Statement, noting, among other themes, "the transformational power of technology".[22]

In sum, the Quad could serve as a role model if it accelerates its proactive efforts and practises its principles and standards by going beyond visions and exhortations. The Quad was originally conceptualised as a security dialogue forum in the 2000s to meet the emerging Chinese opposition to the prevailing world order. A policy-relevant issue is whether the Quad could frame a blueprint for governing critical and emerging technologies besides ensuring the collective security of the original four Indo-Pacific partners.

China's unilateral 'Global Security Initiative' can be compared and contrasted with the Quad's diplomacy of addressing 'soft [non-military] security' issues that might also shape the world's future. Within the Quad, a trilateral military alliance (for practical purposes) is proactive, at this writing, with India remaining a partner of the other Quad members, especially the US.

The Outer Space

Fascinating humanity since ancient times, outer space attracted attention as a new frontier for national security and prosperity following the former Soviet Union's Sputnik launch in 1957. A fair system of global or regional governance of Outer Space remains essential going forward.

The UNGA has indeed adopted an impressive array of space laws. There are five treaties, including the Outer Space Treaty. In addition, five space law principles have been spelt out. The UNGA's 'International Committee on Global Navigation Satellite Systems' also seems to be in place. India, a founding member of the UN, has acceded to the Outer Space Treaty. So, too, PRC, which was admitted to the UN only in 1971, over a quarter century after the UN was founded.

The UN's Conference on Disarmament has also focused attention on preventing an arms race in outer space. However, suspicions among the great and major powers persist. Unsurprising in this context, the US has independently outlined 'Tenets of Responsible Behaviour' in relation to outer space. As an early bird, the US has a space force about which the Chinese complain. Interestingly, Japan has decided to meet the 'China threat' by conceptualising an integrated focus on the space-cyberspace-electromagnetic domains in defence matters.

India and China, too, are proactive space-faring powers. China boasts a full-scope space odyssey, having sent a number of manned space missions and achieved the in-orbit construction of a space station (Tiangong). Beidou is Beijing's own worldwide satellite navigation system, and Yuanwang is the Chinese space-tracking (spy) ship that goes around the world. Potentially, such resourcefulness and resources can also serve the Chinese military aims.

In addition, a series of Beijing's ballistic missile tests, including a suspected hypersonic glide-missile test, has clear military implications. So, too, is that country's anti-satellite test(s). Outwardly, at least, several Chinese lunar probes (including a pioneering voyage to the unseen side of the Moon) and a Mars mission may have been plain scientific projects.

India has a grand space record achieved at a considerably low financial cost compared to the other space-faring majors. The Chandrayaan-1 and Chandrayaan-3 missions, besides the Mangalyaan mission, firmly placed the country in the space super league, especially the successful voyage to Mars in the very first attempt.

Besides scientific feats and the socio-economic usage of a constellation of its own satellites, India has also established a strategic presence in outer space. A series of Agni ballistic missile tests and a successful anti-satellite test confirm the country's preparedness for strategic contingencies.

At a different but related level, the US and India have an accord on space situational awareness, apparently in the civil-military category. More clearly, on the defence side, the two countries have agreed to link their respective space agencies. As if to counterbalance the US-India cooperation, Russia and China collaborate, too. However, the real new storyline is that the Quad has taken the initiative to cooperate. The Quad's 'Working Group on Space Cooperation' could improve the outlook for norm-setting governance of this grey zone, at least on the positive side of the ledger.

This Working Group was set up during the first in-person Quad Leaders' summit in Washington in September 2021. The outer space remained a key focus area of the Quad at its meeting in Hiroshima on May 20, 2023. A question in this overall context is whether India, not just China in Asia, will be among the frontline rule-makers for the governance of this grey zone.

Notes

1.. "The Tallinnn Manual & Primary Law Applicable to Cyber Conflicts", International and Foreign Cyberspace Law Research Guide, *Georgetown Law*, https://guides.ll.georgetown.edu/cyberspace/cyber-conflicts.
2. "About Us", *NATO Cooperative Cyber Defence Centre of Excellence*, https://ccdcoe.org/about-us/.
3. "The NATO CCDCOE welcomes new members Iceland, Ireland, Japan, and Ukraine", *NATO Cooperative Cyber Defence Centre of Excellence*, https://ccdcoe.org/

news/2023/the-nato-ccdcoe-welcomes-new-members-iceland-ireland-japan-and-ukraine/.

4. "Five Eyes Intelligence Oversight and Review Council (FIORC)", *National Counterintelligence and Security Center*, Office of the Director of National Intelligence, https://www.dni.gov/index.php/ncsc-how-we-work/217-about/organization/icig-pages/2660-icig-fiorc.
5. "Full text: Jointly Build a Community with a Shared Future in Cyberspace", State Council, PRC, http://english.scio.gov.cn/whitepapers/2022-11/07/content_78505694_2.htm.
6. Ibid.
7. Ibid.
8. "Priorities for the 78th Session of the United Nations General Assembly", *Ministry of External Affairs*, GOI, https://www.mea.gov.in/India-Priorities-UNGA.htm.
9. "What is GDPR, the EU's new data protection law?", *European Union*, https://gdpr.eu/what-is-gdpr/.
10. "Secretary Antony J. Blinken, Secretary of Defense Lloyd J. Austin III, Indian Minister of External Affairs Dr. S. Jaishankar, and Indian Minister of Defense Rajnath Singh at a Joint Press Availability", *US Department of State*, https://www.state.gov/secretary-antony-j-blinken-secretary-of-defense-lloyd-austin-indian-minister-of-external-affairs-dr-s-jaishankar-and-indian-minister-of-defense-r-ajnath-singh-at-a-joint-press-availability/.
11. "Declaration for the Future of the Internet", *US State Department*, https://www.state.gov/declaration-for-the-future-of-the-internet.
12. "'Explosive' Growth of Digital Technologies Creating New Potential for Conflict, Disarmament Chief Tells Security Council in First-Ever Debate on Cyberthreats", *UN Press*, https://press.un.org/en/2021/sc14563.doc.htm.
13. Ibid.
14. Ibid.
15. Ibid.
16. Chris Miller, *Chip War: The Fight for the World's Most Critical Technology*, Simon & Schuster UK Ltd, London, 2022.
17. Ibid, pp.247—254, also pp. 243—246.
18. "Executive Order on Addressing United States Investments in Certain National Security Technologies and Products in Countries of Concern", *The White House*, https://www.whitehouse.gov/briefing-room/presidential-actions/2023/08/09/executive-order-on-addressing-united-states-investments-in-certain-national-security-technologies-and-products-in-countries-of-concern/.
19. "FACT SHEET: CHIPS and Science Act Will Lower Costs, Create Jobs, Strengthen Supply Chains, and Counter China", *The White House*, https://www.un.org/en/summit-of-the-future#:~:text=22%2D23%20September%202024,Solutions%20for%20a%20Better%20Tomorrow.

20. "Fact Sheet: Quad Leaders' Summit", *The White House*, https://www.whitehouse.gov/briefing-room/statements-releases/2021/09/24/fact-sheet-quad-leaders-summit/.
21. "Quad Principles on Critical and Emerging Technology Standards", *Department of the Prime Minister and Cabinet*, Government of Australia, https://www.pmc.gov.au/resources/quad-principles-critical-and-emerging-technology-standards.
22. "Quad Leaders' Vision Statement - Enduring Partners for the Indo-Pacific", *PM Australia*, https://www.pm.gov.au/media/quad-leaders-vision-statement-enduring-partners-indo-pacific.

7

AI Solution for UNSC Reform: An Idea for a Global AI Order

In geopolitical terms, the global challenges of governing hyper-advanced technologies will remain formidable mainly because the international system is centred on the 'flawed' UNSC. It remains based on the 1945 outcome of World War II. Right now, the flawed UNSC is the only pivotal forum that could, if reformed without bias, ensure the global governance of artificial intelligence (AI), especially its military applications.

Indeed, the escalating development and deployment of AI systems for national military applications are becoming a global concern. It will require a truly unbiased intervention by the UNSC sooner or later. The UNSC must, therefore, be quickly reformed for this emerging reason, among other factors.

The UN knows that it is entrusted with the common and contentious interests of the increasingly divided international community. Furthermore, the rise of new powers has already upset the global order of 1945. However, the UNSC is often paralysed by the powerplays among its five Permanent Members (P5), stakeholders of World War II vintage. The exercise of individual vetoing rights by one or more of the P5 members could kill any unbiased proposal for UNSC reform and global governance of military AI.

Not all the P5 members think alike all the time. The People's Republic of China (PRC) – a P5 member since 1971 (not 1945) – favours the nearly impossible universal consensus for agreeing to any reform proposal.

Debatable is whether this is the PRC's sincere policy to ensure sustainable reform or a subtle ploy to scuttle progress. Due to this factor, the geopolitics of the P5 shapes the UN's ongoing process of evaluating any UNSC reform proposal. Outside of the UN, the chapter will attempt to outline a new idea and later consider whether the P5-geopolitics will promote or prevent the global governance of AI.

Case for Novel AI-Mediated UNSC Reform

Out-of-the-box thinking into the future is needed. A non-partisan AI system could, in my view, suggest a legitimate reconstitution of the UNSC. For that purpose, a customised AI system must be developed and deployed. This can best be done by a non-partisan group of UN-appointed technologists and strategic experts.

Such a mindscape product of AI could be better than a formula which the UN's existing inter-governmental group on UNSC reform is failing to propose. The utter failure of human intelligence in this regard gives room for the deployment of AI to propose a legitimate, fair and practical formula to reform the UNSC. Only a reformed UNSC, reflecting today's actual and tomorrow's likely mosaic of major powers, could credibly try to monitor and regulate the proliferation of AI arms.

It is entirely conceivable that a truly unbiased AI model could indeed propose a non-partisan solution for UNSC reform. Is the deployment of non-partisan AI a strategic imperative for the world at large? Yes. Without a fair reform of the Council, the world's apex security forum, global governance of AI arms (or military applications of AI) will be quite inconceivable.

Above all, human ingenuity has so far failed to evolve a fair formula for UNSC reform. This issue has indeed been discussed, without an outcome, in a relevant forum at the UN for a number of years. Dispassionately, India and several other countries believe that Chinese intransigence is undermining the ongoing process at the UN.

If one or more P5 members remain unwilling to share power with the AI-savvy rising states within a potentially reformed Council, it cannot effectively govern the military applications of AI. This is plain common sense. In fact, a truly reformed UNSC will be essential to ensure a fair and credible global governance of civil AI as well.

Surely, the UN General Assembly (UNGA), comprising all member-states, has a significant role in reflecting international public opinion.

Nonetheless, the P5 members, armed with their individual vetoing power, can directly or indirectly influence the global governance of civil AI, too. As in the nuclear realm, the dual use of AI – for both civil and military purposes – is not inconceivable. In practice, therefore, the simultaneous global governance of both the military and civil AI is needed. This aspect is relevant to the P5, the UNSC as a whole, and the entire UN.

A larger issue is whether the UN and the UNSC have the systemic competence to regulate innovation-driven economic and military activities across the world on a real-time basis. Furthermore, hyper-tech innovations, which require secrecy, cannot be easily regulated. These aspects require an altogether separate study.

The present discussion, however, is justified by the empirical fact that the United Nations and its Security Council are the only institutions with global reach and international agendas. Above all, the UN and its Security Council have already seized several nuances of both civil and military AI (as analysed in earlier chapters).

It is evident, therefore, that a fair AI system, if applied to geopolitics, can catalyse the much-needed systemic reform of the UNSC. Only then will India and the other deserving countries get their legitimate say in global affairs. These matters include the global governance of hyper-advanced tech domains. Paradoxically, this will also be a case of using non-partisan AI to build a new UNSC to govern all aspects of AI, too!

The Process of AI Solution: A Scenario

Who can initiate the process of AI-mediated UNSC reform, and how? The answer is the UN Secretary-General, regardless of the primacy (or otherwise) of the person holding this office at any given time vis-à-vis the P5 members individually and collectively. Two interrelated aspects – the UNSC reform and the global AI governance – are at stake.

Relevant to this context is the importance of the following announcement by UN Secretary-General Antonio Guterres on October 26, 2023. Addressing the media in New York, Guterres said, “Today I am launching my High-Level Multistakeholder Advisory Body on Artificial Intelligence”. Two points stood out. First, he had clearly taken the initiative in this regard, with or without the consent of the P5 members. Second, equally clear was his decision to set up an advisory body or panel, not a decision-making authority.

Similarly, the UN Secretary-General could set up an advisory panel consisting of a few unbiased AI technologists. They must be mandated to evolve a non-partisan AI model (or system) and train it by using authentic data about the evolution of the UN and UNSC. Such data should include the attitude of each existing P5 member towards the issue of UNSC reform. Another crucial feedstock for training this AI model would be the unbiased narrative about each rising power that wants to be a new permanent member of the UNSC. Specifically, the data feed for the AI model must cover the aspiring rising powers' respective capabilities to be responsible new permanent members of the UNSC.

What should the unbiased AI technologists and their non-partisan AI model do? Technologists will be expected to train their AI model to study the huge amount of relevant data very closely. In the follow-on sequential steps, the AI system should be guided or trained to learn and think. As a result, the model could acquire either guided autonomy or self-learnt autonomy, depending on the scope of the technologists' software. After that stage is reached, the AI system would, in all probability, outline a roadmap for the UNSC reform.

Depending on the mandate for the technologists, the AI solution could include the overall UN reforms as well. A significant point to be noted is that the scenario (described here) is for securing an AI-mediated advisory roadmap, especially for UNSC reform. Decision-making on the basis of such an advisory roadmap will be the geopolitical prerogative of the UN member-states. A peep at the geopolitics of major powers at the UN, including the P5 members in particular, will be instructive to understand the current limits to innovative UN reforms.

Instead of being a figment of hilarious unrealism, AI-mediated reform may be a good bet for the UNSC. It is high time the UNSC kept pace with the geopolitical realities of the 21st century. Nonetheless, at this writing, dim indeed is the creative prospect of a non-partisan AI system being developed to reform the UN's premier organ.

Numerous the objections. First, the P5 members cannot be expected to agree to rock their comfortable boat. They will not accept an uncertain future for them at the outset of a conceivable AI-mediated UNSC reform process. Second, the search for algorithm designers and AI system developers – with no personal or national bias – will be like going to the Moon, in the old metaphor for unalloyed pessimism.

Significantly, the US, Russia, China and India have reached and explored the Moon in their respective high-science and hyper-tech endeavours. On a moonlit night in Beijing, a friend teased me, saying that I was staring at an artificial Moon crafted and put in orbit by China! Indeed, China's astronomical reputation for hyper-tech capabilities is astronomical. The question, however, is whether China will be willing to consider the hyper-tech proposition of AI-mediated UNSC reform in the context of the utter failure of human ingenuity.

China's Consensus Strategy

Beijing's perceived intransigence, at this writing, is a substantive reason for the failure of the UN's relevant inter-governmental panel to evolve a formula for the UNSC reform. In the divisive geopolitics, until at least mid-2024, China has been demanding universal consensus in all but name. Often, Beijing propagates its demand for universal consensus in a subtle manner.

On February 29, in the leap year of 2024, Chinese spokeswoman Mao Ning explicitly addressed the issue as, "The reform of the Security Council is an integral part of the reform of the UN as a whole... Member-states need to seek the broadest possible consensus for a package solution through serious and thorough consultations. The reform should benefit all member-states".[1]

It is arguable that the broadest possible consensus is not the same as universal consensus. Nevertheless, universal consensus, especially on critical issues, is implied in her qualifying comment about the need to ensure benefit for all member-states. In a subtle message, she left it unsaid that the broadest possible consensus, without all member-states being party to it, would not necessarily benefit all.

In effect, universal consensus would be required to ensure universal benefit, especially on critical issues like regional or global security in the development and deployment of AI arms. An enlightened alternative to universal consensus on such issues would be an effective maximal majority vote in the UNSC.

For this alternative to be realised, the states armed with individual vetoing rights will have to suspend their respective prerogative of exercising that right. In particular, the Privileged Five (as the P5 is) will have to suspend, if not give up, their respective vetoing right on critical issues like AI arms. This is a very, very tall order, to say the least (See also the Annex).

However, the PRC had already reaped its harvest by gaining entry into the UN and the UNSC through a viable alternative to universal consensus in 1971. PRC unseated its predecessor, the Republic of China (ROC), at the UN in that year, with the UNGA adopting a relevant resolution.[2] In effect, the mandatory amendment of the UN Charter was bypassed. (The UN Charter still carries the name of ROC as a permanent member of the UNSC).

In this light, China is aware that India's and a few others' valid credentials for permanent membership in the UNSC need not necessarily be tested for universal consensus. Nonetheless, even in the 21st century ambience, Beijing has been propagating the idea of universal consensus, either openly or in a subtle manner. By doing so, Beijing has effectively blocked India and a few other deserving countries like Germany and Japan.

Furthermore, Mao Ning, responding to questions from an Indian journalist on February 29, 2024, noted the following: "The [UNSC] reform should benefit all member-states, rather than serving the selfish interests of a few [like India, Germany and Japan]". Nonetheless, to erase the impression of a Freudian slip about protecting the selfish interests of the P5 members (especially China), she added: "I don't think that the Security Council only represents the interests of the permanent members".[3] Above all, Xi's commitment to sustain the 1945 international order into the distant future has been absolutely explicit in the public domain. Before the September 2024 UN Summit of the Future, there was no indication that China and Russia would want the unrepresentative UNSC to be reformed urgently. This negative aspect casts a shadow into the future over the much-needed global governance of AI and the cyber-digital domain.

Relevant to this reality is the anecdote about China's evident tactic to humour India while actually hurting the latter's interests as well as those of the wider world. Recalling a visit to Delhi in April 2005 by the-then Chinese Premier Wen Jiabao to balance an emerging US-India entente, India's then Foreign Secretary Shyam Saran later narrated this: "Wen Jiabao even conveyed China's support for India's claim to [permanent] membership of the UN Security Council but said that he could not declare this publicly since China could not support [its adversary] Japan's candidature".[4]

A smart Chinese ploy par excellence because Japan, Germany, India and Brazil had already come together as aspirants for UNSC permanent membership in the 21st century. These four countries and a few others continue to be relevant to any democratic process of shaping a new world order. Their non-inclusion as UNSC's permanent members, at this writing, will only reduce or nullify the effectiveness of this apex security forum for global governance of grey zones like AI.

The Democratic 'Option' for Reform

Significantly, the democratic process of UN reforms is said to be China's preferred course, although the mantra of consensus has not been given up. Addressing the international media in Beijing on March 7, 2024, Chinese Foreign Minister Wang Yi said: "Taking international rule of law as the basis, fairness and justice as a principle, win-win cooperation as the goal and effective action as an orientation, we will practise true multilateralism and promote greater democracy and rule of law in international relations".[5]

What does democracy in international relations mean? Insightfully, it cannot imply universal consensus among all UN members on any (or a specific) issue. The essence of democracy is fair debate that enables all relevant parties to decide on the basis of views or votes among the majority of these stakeholders. It is common sense, therefore, that China's idea of consensus among all stakeholders is incompatible with the democratic practice of ascertaining the majority views and/or votes.

A solid reason is that China's subtle advocacy of universal consensus if it is to be a decision-making imperative, would give each UN member-state undeclared vetoing rights. This would, in effect, complicate the process of UN reforms. Not only that. Without reforms for power-sharing among major members, it would be difficult for the UN system to enforce its will in the hyper-advanced technology domains like AI and cyberspace.

Decision-making on the basis of a majority of votes – a practice at the UN, too – may not necessarily meet the political will of every member-state. To accommodate the interests of the maximal number of member-states, special majority votes – two-thirds (66.66%), three-fourths (75%), four-fifths (80%) or even nine-tenths (90%) – could be considered on a case-by-case basis. By accepting the higher margins of the majority, I think China could actually promote greater democracy at the UN on emergency issues of the future, like AI and cyberspace.

The issue of voting majorities for democratic decision-making at the UN on sensitive aspects of AI and the cyber-digital domains may attain practical importance sooner or later. In view of the Digital Compact, which, at this writing, is a work in progress, civil and military dimensions of the high-tech grey zones could come into sharp focus. The Interim Report of the 'UN AI Advisory Body', released on December 21, 2023, was an early signpost towards potential, but not definitive, global governance of AI.

An Avenue Towards a Global AI Order

AI is the high-tech flavour of the times as the clock ticks relentlessly in this 21st century. Positive expectations and negative concerns about AI have already come to the fore during the UNGA's debates, respectively, on the civil and military dimensions of this technology. Above all, the perceptions of AI as the potential enabler of massively destructive autonomous weapons have already shaken the world to its core.

There is a growing realisation that AI's capabilities to power hyper-destructive weapons, if not properly regulated into the future, might be more dangerous than the most powerful nuclear weapons. Even the most lethal nuclear arsenals have remained under human control as of this writing. The tech characteristics of AI systems, including their self-learning capabilities to become autonomous of human control, have, therefore, come under scrutiny. Human control over AI systems under institutional framework(s) has become a serious imperative.

A brief reality check would show up a grim scenario. 'Frontier AI' models could enable the functioning of autonomous weapons-grade devices with the potential to unleash unimaginable destruction. Some policymakers, administrators, and sensitive people have begun to think about ways to mitigate the dangers of such AI-powered devices. The worst-case scenario is that of state(s) and even non-state actor(s) developing and deploying such devices. A point to remember in this scenario is that 'Frontier AI' could be a tech enabler of such self-learning weapon systems. (See Annex also)

Unsurprisingly, UN Secretary General Antonio Guterres was among the first leaders to voice support for administering AI under a credible institutional arrangement. Speaking at the UNSC first-ever debate on AI on July 18, 2023, Guterres stated that, "First, powerful AI models are already widely available to the general public. Second, unlike nuclear material and chemical and biological agents, AI tools can be moved around the world, leaving very little trace. Third, the private sector's leading role in AI has few parallels in other strategic technologies… I agree with the large number of experts that have recommended the prohibition of lethal autonomous weapons [that could operate] without human control".[6]

Obviously aware of the complex geopolitics of prohibiting such weapons in this AI age, Guterres proposed exploring the feasibility of an institutional arrangement for the governance of AI. He, therefore, endorsed the "calls from some member states for the creation of a new United Nations entity to support collective efforts to govern this extraordinary technology".[7] Those calls, he told the UNSC, were "inspired by such models as the International Atomic Energy Agency (IAEA), the International Civil Aviation Organization (ICAO) or the Intergovernmental Panel on Climate Change".[8]

Setting out the mandate for such an institution, Guterres said, "The overarching goal of this body would be to support countries to maximize the benefits of AI for good, to mitigate existing and potential risks, and to establish and administer internationally agreed mechanisms of monitoring and governance".[9] The proposition was specific about an existing model as an example that could be followed, but it was vague on the means to address the military applications of AI.

Institutional Control of AI Arms

A critical issue that must be addressed is the perceived potential of frontier AI technology to enable futurist autonomous weapons to cause unimaginable destruction. An imperative, I think, is the creation of a non-partisan international institution to address the concerns about AI arms. At stake are the potential weapons of mass destruction powered by this hyper-advanced technology.

An AI-arms-control institution, if launched, could supplement the IAEA-like entity that Guterres endorsed for the civil side of AI. At this writing, the IAEA-like civil-AI entity and my idea of a non-partisan international institution/mechanism for AI arms control have not been accepted by the UN or any coalition. Nonetheless, the conceptualisation of this magnitude merits attention.

Surveying the AI landscape in the first quarter of the 21st century, Sinologist Henry Kissinger suggested substantive US-China engagement on AI arms control (Chapter 5). He reckoned that the US and China were already AI superpowers. Unsurprising, US Secretary of State Antony Blinken said, after meeting President Xi in Beijing on April 26, 2024, that the previously planned US-China talks on AI would be held.[10]

At least one round of US-China talks on AI has been held, as of this writing, in mid-2024. However, this notion of a US-China AI-G2 (Group of Two) cannot meaningfully form the basis for the creation of an AI-arms-control institution or mechanism. The reasoning is simple but significant.

The Nuclear Non-Proliferation Treaty (NPT), founded on the basis of exclusive rights for five designated states with atomic arsenals, has not created a non-partisan nuclear world order. Moreover, the US-Soviet Union dialogue on their strategic arms during the now-bygone Cold War is not an ideal model for the present- and future worlds of multiple powers. (The enormous evidence regarding the NPT and the Cold War strategic 'logic' is outside the scope of this book.)

Kissinger's classification of the US and China, in that order, as the exclusive AI superpowers, cannot create a non-partisan international institution to control AI arms. These two countries seem to be ahead of their respective competitors in technological progress, research funding, and so on, especially in the realm of military AI. Nonetheless, several other countries – India, Japan, and some European powers – are also AI-savvy and have AI competence in both civil and military domains.

The lurking danger in Kissinger's proposition is that it could lead to an NPT-like discriminatory AI order. Such a denouement will be unfair to the world at large, not just India or other AI-savvy countries. India is developing its AI-armed deterrence capabilities in a quest for a strategic edge over the adversaries (Chapter 1).

In both the civil and military domains of AI, China does not take its eyes off the US and vice versa. However, quoting Chinese sources, a researcher has noted that "the computing power of the entire country of China is not comparable to that of a single US tech giant".[11] With a US company achieving a breakthrough in creating a text-to-video AI model, China is trying to "propel [AI] innovation in the global landscape"[12] to counter the US.

Relevant to this US-China contest (and the potential India-China equation) is the view at the UNGA about two indispensable principles – responsibility in using AI arms under intelligent human control. Furthermore, China has emphasised the "dual-use nature of AI technology" and called for respect for "international humanitarian law [law of war] and other applicable international laws".[13]

International law and the US-conceptualised rules-based international order are increasingly seen as relevant (or otherwise) to global governance, including in the sphere of AI. John Dugard, former Member of the International Law Commission, has emphasised the contentious nature of the rules-based international order.

John Dugard wrote, "Charitably, it may be seen as an order comprising values of a liberal order. Less charitably, it may be seen as a competing order advocated by some Western states, particularly the United States, which seeks to impose the interpretation of international law that best advances the interests of the West, particularly those of the United States. Unlike international law, it does not seem to be a universal order. It is an order employed by the West, again particularly the United States, to ensure its dominance".[14]

China has been challenging the perceived US agenda and calling for "a universal international regime" for the governance of AI. In this ambience, India has a unique democratic role to play to ensure a fair AI order.

Notes

1. "Foreign Ministry Spokesperson Mao Ning's Regular Press Conference on February 29, 2024", *Ministry of Foreign Affairs*, PRC, https://www.fmprc.gov.cn/eng/xwfw_665399/s2510_665401/2511_665403/202402/t20240229_11252090.html.
2. "U.N. Resolution 2758 (U.N. Voted To Admit Communist China, Expel Nationalist Delegates.)" *American Institute in Taiwan*, https://web-archive-2017.ait.org.tw/en/un-res-2758-voted-to-admit-communist-china.html.
3. n.1. Answering journalist KJM Varma's question.
4. Shyam Saran, *How China Sees India and the World*, (New Delhi, India: Juggernaut Books, 2022), pp. 201-202.
5. "Member of the Political Bureau of the CPC Central Committee and Foreign Minister Wang Yi Meets the Press" *Ministry of Foreign Affairs*, PRC, https://www.fmprc.gov.cn/eng/zxxx_662805/202403/t20240307_11255682.html.
6. "Secretary-General Urges Security Council to Ensure Transparency, Accountability, Oversight, in First Debate on Artificial Intelligence", *UN*, https://press.un.org/en/2023/sgsm21880.doc.htm.
7. Ibid.
8. Ibid.
9. Ibid.

10. "Secretary Antony J. Blinken at a Press Availability - United States Department of State", *US Department of State*, https://www.state.gov/secretary-antony-j-blinken-at-a-press-availability-48/.
11. Shan Wei, "Sora's Surge: China's AI Race Heats Up in Response to OpenAI's Latest Breakthrough", *EAI Commentary*, No. 78, 2 May 2024, East Asian Institute, National University of Singapore, http://research.nus.edu.sg.
12. Ibid. A more advanced AI innovation, Generative Pre-Trained Transformer (GPT-4o), has followed 'Sora', at this writing. This is just an illustrative example, not an exhaustive example of the ongoing AI innovations.
13. PRC's Mission to the UN Office at Geneva (Already referenced).
14. John Dugard, "The choice before us: International law or a 'rules-based international order'? *Leiden Journal of International Law*, Published online by Cambridge University Press.

8

Mosaic of AI Governance Outside the UN Framework

While the UN remains the premier forum, with a global reach, for rule-making in the governance of AI and the cyber-digital domain, regional and functional groups, too, play important roles. Of such groups, the China-led Belt and Road Forum (BRF) – a connectivity-oriented group – has, we have seen, set for itself an authoritarian model of AI governance. This can be traced to China's domineering presence and leadership within the BRF. However, the attitudes of China's partner countries might become clear in due course.

As a compact four-state Indo-Pacific group disliked by China – the Quad – appears to have been a pioneer in identifying minute details of "critical and emerging technologies". However, the group – led by the US and including two of its military allies (Japan and Australia) and one strategic partner (India) – seems to cast the technological net very wide. Furthermore, the Quad members are still at the stage of conceptualising principles and articulating vision rather than formulating viable standards. The four countries are active in other groups as well.

At the third in-person Quad summit, hosted by Australia in Hiroshima (Japan) on May 20, 2023, the leaders issued the 'Quad Principles on Critical and Emerging Technology Standards'. The statement was more generic than specific: "We affirm our support for inclusive practices such as the use of diverse and inclusive data sets in the field of artificial intelligence to encourage the development of technology standards that take into account diverse views and voices".[1] In a broader sweep, the leaders agreed to "foster technology standards that support safety, security and resilience". Standards for the use of AI, even within the confines of Quad, were not negotiated.

As Lead Chair of the 'Global Partnership on Artificial Intelligence' (GPAI) for the year 2024, India convened a meeting of this forum in New Delhi on December 13, 2023. The Indian agenda for 2024 was spelt out at the meeting mentioned above. Issues concerning GPAI members' access to "critical resources for AI research and innovation" were identified at the Delhi meeting ahead of the forum's activities in 2024. At that meeting, the GPAI Ministers expressed support for India's emphasis on access to research-facilitating resources "in compliance with applicable intellectual property protections and data protection legislations".[2]

An important nuance to be noted is the following. As discussed in Chapters 4 and 5, India does not share China's view that national sovereignty is the eternal, inviolable red line when considering AI matters. While cherishing national sovereignty, Delhi does recognise AI as a borderless domain that could extend to outer space.

However, in the GPAI forum with a diverse membership, India advocates for access to research-promoting resources in compliance with "applicable... protections and... legislations". This messaging is as good a code as any for the sovereignty of each country over the AI-research-enabling resources within its borders and jurisdictions. Such a balancing act by India also illustrates the complexities of governing or administering AI at the level of the UN or coalitions like the GPAI.

At the GPAI's Delhi meeting, the AI-research-developing resources were identified: "AI computing, high-quality, diverse datasets, algorithms, software, testbeds, and other AI-relevant resources".[3] Overall, at the meeting India had convened, GPAI affirmed its "commitment to continue to work within our respective [national] jurisdictions to advance safe, secure, and trustworthy AI".[4]

Under India's presidency of the Group of Twenty (G20) major economies, in 2023, an agreement was reached on the imperative of ethical use of AI (briefly in Chapter 4). Besides India, the US, China, Japan, and some European powers are among the G20 members.

An aspirational AI Statement on "Principles for responsible stewardship of trustworthy AI"[5] was issued by the G20 at its Osaka summit in Japan in

2019. Outlining a grand wish list, as it were, the G20 called on all relevant stakeholders to promote "inclusive growth, sustainable development and well-being" with a steady focus on "people and the planet".

To promote "human-centred values and fairness", the G20 said that "AI actors should respect the rule of law, human rights and democratic values, throughout the AI system lifecycle". Left unsaid by the G20 but well-known is the political divide within the group on the true meaning of democratic values.

Beijing's grandstanding on democracy with Chinese characteristics may amuse the US, which prides itself as the world's oldest democracy, and India, the acknowledged largest democracy. On a different aspect of AI principles, the AI actors were urged by the G20 to "commit [themselves] to transparency and responsible disclosure regarding AI systems".[6]

G20's Key 'Recommendation'

Worth noting in the G20's wish list is the advocacy for "fostering a digital ecosystem for AI" in the member countries of this group and beyond. As the cyber-digital domains constitute the core platform for AI development and deployment, the advocacy for a digital ecosystem for AI is very apt indeed. There was no specific suggestion that the proposed ecosystem be globalised. The G20's Statement identified characteristics of the AI-specific ecosystem: "digital technologies and infrastructure, and mechanisms for sharing AI knowledge, as appropriate".[7]

Amplifying the idea of AI knowledge sharing across national borders, the G20 Statement ran as follows: "Governments should consider promoting mechanisms, such as data trusts, to support the safe, fair, legal and ethical sharing of data".[8] While this proposition is conceptually sound, all countries, especially major economies and political powerhouses, will look at data sharing, among many issues, through the lenses of national security and sovereignty.

It can be inferred, in this context, that the G20's condition of appropriate sharing translates into a guideline for safeguarding national sovereignty and security while sharing data, etc. Such a limit on sharing is not confined to China or India. No country in the G20 will be willing to part with sensitive data without due diligence. But, as we know, China has already elevated its national sovereignty in the AI-cyber-digital domains to the status of a red line that should not be trifled with. Furthermore, Beijing advocates for the inviolability of any country's national sovereignty in global high-tech transactions.

Paradoxically, however, Beijing is red in the face over Washington's efforts to safeguard its national security by banning or curbing the exports of US-origin high-tech semiconductors to China. In a phone conversation on April 2, 2024, Chinese President Xi told his US counterpart, Joe Biden, that Washington's high-tech curbs on Beijing would only cause a two-way risk. It would not help Washington to de-risk its trade-and-tech ties with Beijing, in turn Xi warned that "China is not going to sit back and watch".[9] For Beijing, obviously, there is a fine difference between American national security and Chinese national sovereignty[10] , which is laced with national security.

As far back as July 2017, China called for the development of AI at home to "maintain national security". Outlining a comprehensive set of objectives, China's State Council emphasised that "AI should be applied in national defence, including military command, equipment and drills".[11] Indeed, for all independent countries, the pre-condition for attaining national security is the exercise of national sovereignty. In the Sino-American equation, it is significant, therefore, that Beijing clearly values the old idiom that "what is good for the goose is not good for the gander".

Norms of AI Governance

Amid expectations and scepticism about progress towards the formulation of norms for the global governance of AI, the UN AI Advisory Body launched its Interim Report. In the UN's plan of action, the final report, which has not yet been released when this is written, was expected to stimulate the outcome of the September 2024 Summit of the Future.

Summarising the Interim Report, the UN said in a press release on December 21, 2023 that the Advisory Body "calls for grounding artificial intelligence in universal principles". This meant that AI, despite its phenomenal advancement as a vibrant hyper-tech innovation, should be treated like all other technological inventions for its use under human control. Also outlined in the report were "tasks for a potential institution on AI governance".[12]

Concerned about the risks that AI's unimaginable potential could trigger, the advisory body called for a thorough scanning of possibilities in this regard. To mitigate risks, the panel suggested international collaboration on data. Several other aspects of international collaboration were also emphasised with a view to enabling the UN system to accomplish the Sustainable Development Goals as planned. Overall, "an equitable voice for all countries" and the need to "empower the Global South" on all AI matters were advocated.[13]

Key principles for building global AI-governance institutions were spelt out in the interim report. These norms, as advocated by the panel, included inclusivity of citizens across the world (encompassing the Global South of developing countries as well). Closely linked to this principle, AI governance institutions should uphold the public interest. The promotion of data commons and data governance would facilitate global AI governance. It was further suggested that AI-savvy countries and stakeholders should universalise the governance of this technology. Above all, AI governance system(s) must function within the bounds of international law. The UN Charter, the International Humanitarian Law and the Sustainable Development Goals were identified by the panel as some of the benchmarks for global AI governance under international law.[14]

The final report of the UN AI Advisory Body, a major input for the UN Summit of the Future, scheduled on September 22-23 2024, was not released by mid-2024. Nonetheless, the well-known indisputable principles for the governance of AI might be practised on the basis of the calculus of power at the national, regional and global levels. There is already a school of thought – bracketing the US and China, in that order, as the only two AI superpowers. A real or notional US-China Artificial Intelligence-Group of Two (AI-G2) at the helm of global governance of AI could be a divisive game. Major AI-savvy countries, including India, must be at the high table of AI governance. This will be the best bet for a bright future.

Notes

1. "Quad Principles on Critical and Emerging Technology Standards", *Ministry of External Affairs*, GoI, https://www.mea.gov.in/bilateral-documents.htm?dtl/36575/quad+principles+on+critical+and+emerging+technology+standards#:~:text=We%20affirm%20our%20support%20for%20inclusive%20practices%20such%20as%20the-,support%20safety%2C%20security%20and%20resilience.
2. "GPAI Ministerial Declaration 2023", *The Global Partnership on Artificial Intelligence*, https://gpai.ai/2023-GPAI-Ministerial-Declaration.pdf.
3. Ibid.

4. Ibid.
5. "G20 AI Principles", *Ministry of Foreign Affairs*, Government of Japan, https://www.mofa.go.jp/policy/economy/g20_summit/osaka19/pdf/documents/en/annex_08.pdf.
6. Ibid.
7. Ibid.
8. Ibid.
9. "President Xi Jinping Speaks with U.S. President Joe Biden on the Phone", Ministry of Foreign Affairs, PRC, https://www.fmprc.gov.cn/eng/zxxx_662805/202404/t20240403_11275451.html.
10. As referenced in Chapter 3, "national sovereignty" figured as a key principle in the "Global AI Governance Initiative" which China unveiled in October 2023.
11. Referenced in Chapter 3.
12. "UN AI Advisory Body calls for grounding artificial intelligence in universal principles, suggests tasks for a potential institution on AI governance", *UN Press*, https://www.un.org/sites/un2.un.org/files/un_ai_advisory_body_interim_report_press_release.pdf.
13. "Interim Report: Governing AI for Humanity", *United Nations*, https://www.un.org/en/ai-advisory-body#:~:text=The%20UN%20Secretary%2DGeneral%27s%20AI,is%20developed%20and%20rolled%20out
14. Ibid.

9

Summary and Conclusions: AI Geopolitics by Mid-2024

As a premier fast-evolving innovation of our times, AI is a key topic on the agenda of the UN Summit of the Future, scheduled for September 22-23, 2024. In fact, AI is widely seen as the technological domain that could determine the global pecking order of powerful and influential countries.

Humanity's New Destiny

Aspiring to be a good globalist, almost every member-state in the UN recognises the acceptance of the unique AI as humanity's new destiny. This robust attitude explains the unanimous adoption of two separate civil AI resolutions by the UNGA. Of these two resolutions, the first, piloted by the US on "Safe, Secure And Trustworthy" AI, was adopted on March 21, 2024. India, a key partner of the US, was privy to the consultative process behind the scenes.

The second Civil AI Resolution, crafted by China on international cooperation for building the AI-related capacity of developing countries, was adopted on July 1, 2024. The theme in a non-binding resolution was unexceptionable for all. It is entirely left to the discretion of the UN member-states to implement or ignore these two resolutions. However, as they reflect international public opinion, the emerging US-China tussle for leadership or even hegemony in the global AI domain must be watched.

A Non-Binding UNGA Resolution on AI Arms

The resolution adopted on December 22, 2023 – the first of any UNGA resolution on AI – addressed the challenges and concerns raised by autonomous weapons systems. India was among the few countries that voted against that resolution. China abstained from voting, while the US voted for it. India stated its consistent view, emphasising the need to strike a "balance between military necessity and humanitarian imperatives". In Delhi's subtle view, such a balance was not achieved in that resolution. Both India and China were not in favour of the UNGA duplicating the ongoing efforts in this regard under the framework of the UN's own Convention on Certain Conventional Weapons. China had already unveiled its own Global AI Governance Initiative in October 2023. With that benchmark in mind, Beijing abstained from voting. The US issued a "Political Declaration on Responsible Military Use of Artificial Intelligence and Autonomy" on November 9, 2023. Besides, the US, facing international pressure for supporting Israel in the Gaza War at that time, backed the resolution that was in sync with the global humanitarian concerns.

With both the civil and military applications of AI, especially Frontier AI (the most advanced AI), coming into sharp focus by mid-2024, the India-China, India-US, and China-US equations require close attention.

India-China AI Race

Competitive nationalism in the complicated Sino-Indian geostrategic ties. India's aim is to become a global leader in AI innovation. Delhi's regional and global diplomacy on AI issues appears to be evolving at this writing. China's aim is to be a global innovation centre by 2030. Overall, Beijing seems keen to globalise its AI brand and contribute to the world as a superpower in all aspects of AI.

India's emerging AI doctrine is non-threatening globalism, centred on AI innovation for a start. China appears keen to exercise its sovereignty as a global AI leader or hegemon and to try to shape the shared future of all countries. A sign of Beijing's emerging AI doctrine is the Shanghai Declaration on Global AI Governance issued at a Chinese-led World AI Conference on July 4, 2024.[1] This document advocates for a global scope governance mechanism to "ensure the safety, controllability and reliability of AI technologies". Another aspect of Beijing's potential AI doctrine is reflected in the Chinese-crafted UNGA resolution of July 1, 2024 – helping developing countries in their AI capacity-building.[2]

The IndiaAI Mission, approved on March 7, 2024, is a public-private partnership model for five years, with an intended funding of over Rs. 10,000 crores. The aim is to build a robust AI innovation ecosystem. China's State Council has set a target for the value of cumulative output of Chinese AI industries. The aim is to exceed US$150 billion by 2030. India's quest for AI-enabled national defence was articulated by Prime Minister Narendra Modi in July 2022. In his view, "it is crucial to promote customisation and uniqueness of our defence systems for a strategic edge over the adversaries". Beijing had, in 2017, floated its Artificial Intelligence Development Plan (AIDP). A punchline of the AIDP revealed Beijing's intention to "apply AI to China's national defence". The name of the military game in China, at this writing, is "the development and utilisation of new types of combat forces". Foremost among these new types, as identified by Chinese President and Chairman of the Central Military Commission, Xi Jinping, is AI-powered combat forces, i.e. weapon systems.

On the other hand, India has adopted an internal policy of democratisation of technology, including in the AI space. In the socio-economic sector, the Digital Public Infrastructure (DPI) is focused on corruption-free direct delivery of public services to eligible beneficiaries. Encouraged by the perceived success of this massive effort, India has projected the DPI as a globally replicable public good and offered to help other developing countries. China is propagating the idea of technology transfer from AI-savvy powers to developing countries for capacity-building in this domain. China's own action in this regard will be watched closely.

India has been ranked 15 out of 25 top-ranked AI nations. An empirical scorecard prepared by Fletcher School in the US shows China in the second position below the US itself at the peak. China will seek to leverage its high rank and try to shape a global AI order. However, India could also seek to play a significant role in building the same AI order. Analysing the Fletcher School's findings, Harvard Business Review emphasised that India is the one with the greatest upward potential in the AI domain. China may have taken note.

India has the policy option of seeking mutually beneficial technological cooperation with the advanced US. China cannot competitively turn towards another advanced technological power, especially if India could enhance its ties with Russia, Beijing's best bet in mid-2024. The Sino-Indian AI race does not need to be a zero-sum game. China seeks to helm global affairs in artificial intelligence. India is pursuing a calibrated path upwards, beginning with AI innovation. This race may, therefore, centre on the core issue of AI innovation, at least for a start.

Indeed, some compatibility in the Sino-Indian views relate mainly to (1) human control over, and human responsibility for, AI arms; (2) the relevance of International Humanitarian Law (the law of war) and, broadly, international law; and (3) the continuing importance of discussions and/or negotiations on AI, within the Group of Governmental Experts' framework at the United Nations (under the existing Convention on Certain Conventional Weapons).

India-US Collaboration

Prime Minister Modi and US President Joe Biden announced, in May 2022, an exclusive US-India Initiative on Critical and Emerging Technologies (iCET), which took off in January 2023. For a start, Biden identified a target of harnessing our shared expertise on quantum computing and artificial intelligence.

On June 17, 2024, National Security Adviser Ajit Doval and his US counterpart Jake Sullivan held a second meeting under the iCET framework in New Delhi. It was noted that the two sides "have made significant strides towards deepening and expanding strategic cooperation across key technology sectors, including... artificial intelligence".[3] Bilateral collaboration in the domains of "quantum, artificial intelligence, and high-performance computing" is being pursued. Significant is the disclosure that the US Administration "continues to work with the US Congress to lower barriers to US exports to India for high-performance computing and source code".

Signifying intensified US-India engagement in the high-tech domains, the two sides held talks at the Pentagon in May 2024 under the framework of Advanced Domains Defence Dialogue (AD3). A table-top exercise on space-related cooperation was held. Another feature was the focus on AI, among other emerging domains, during the bilateral expert exchanges under the AD3 process.[4] The technological spin-offs from the discussions under the iCET and AD3 processes will be known if and when this bilateral engagement matures in a big way in due course.

It is an open question whether India would acquire AI arms from the US as a result of the iCET and AD3 processes. In the public domain, there is no evidence that India might have already acquired such capabilities through 'technology transfer' from the US. At the other end of the spectrum, the US itself seems to regard India as a competent technology partner in the military AI realm. Much will also depend on how the global geopolitics concerning the US, India, China and Russia evolves going forward. In particular, India's engagements with Russia and China, in that order, will be closely watched by Washington.

US-China AI Rivalry

In December 2023, Harvard Business Review noted that the US and China were engaged in a digital cold war to be the world's top AI economy. The observation was based on the Fletcher School's empirical study that resulted in a list of top-ranked AI nations. The US and China emerged as the first and second AI powers. Certainly, the notion of a US-China digital cold war is gaining credibility, but a pragmatic truce is not entirely ruled out.

On the strategic turf, the US has styled itself as "a global leader in the responsible development and use of weapon systems with autonomous functions", notably AI arms. In November 2023 (as noted above), the US State Department issued a political declaration on responsible military use of AI. Long accustomed to being the world's most powerful military player, the US wants to appear a responsible leader rather than asking the entire world to be good. In contrast, China has resorted to grandstanding and sermonising as a global mentor and tries to conceal its targeted verbal attacks on the US.

China submitted to the UN, on December 13, 2021, a paper on "Regulating Military Applications of Artificial Intelligence". While being replete with dos and don'ts for the world at large, China's verbal attack on the US was in much-understood coded language – "[All] countries need to bear in mind that military applications of AI shall never be used as a tool to start a war or pursue hegemony. We [the Chinese] oppose moves to undermine the sovereignty and territorial security of other countries [such as China] by using advantages in AI technology [such as America's]". Was China responding to US Defence Secretary Lloyd Austin's candid statement, on July 13, 2021, on the Chinese AI profile. Austin had said as follows: "In the

AI realm as in many others, we [the Americans] understand that China is our pacing challenge. We're going to compete to win, but we are going to do it the right way". The battle lines for the US-China cold war in the realm of AI, especially on the strategic turf, are drawn.

AI is not the monopoly of any state or non-state actor. However, the US and China have begun to act as if they hold the trump card to lead. In this writing, the European Union and India are prominent among the other players to watch. But the US-China rivalry hogs the headlines.

UN – the 'Go-to-place' for AI Governance

Amazing is the pace at which advancements in the domain of artificial intelligence are taking place. By mid-2024, 'Frontier AI'[5] has almost become a substantive buzzword.

Coalitions like the Quad and multilateral forums like the G20 address the challenges of administering AI. However, the UN, with its convening power, is the forum of choice for many countries for the governance of AI in the global commons. How does the UN's progress card look in this regard?

The ongoing saga began at the UN on July 18, 2023. During the UNSC first-ever debate on AI on that day, UN Secretary-General Antonio Guterres urged the "prohibition of lethal autonomous weapons [which are deployable] without human control". A tall order in the global commons but still in vogue in debating circles.

With breathtaking AI advancements taking place, Guterres launched a "High-Level Multistakeholder Advisory Body on Artificial Intelligence" (AI Advisory Body) in New York on October 26, 2023. The Interim Report, submitted by the AI Advisory Body on December 21, 2023, called for "grounding artificial intelligence in universal principles". This means that AI, a truly unique innovation, should be treated like all other technologies to assess its impact on the well-being and progress of the entire human society. Another tall order in the global commons. The AI Advisory Body's final report, a key input for the UN Summit of the Future on September 22-23, 2024, was not released at this writing.

In international relations, though, principles can be practised only within a global, regional or even national calculus of power. In this context, the US identified democracy as the heartbeat of AI algorithms (in metaphoric terms). For India, it seems, the heartbeat of AI algorithms is induced by the advancements of this technology itself. For Beijing, the heartbeat of AI algorithms must be in sync with the Chinese national sovereignty.

A major geopolitical category, according to Sinologist Henry Kissinger, consists of the US and China as the only two AI superpowers. However, they are not the only countries with substantial AI capabilities and aspirations. As a rising AI power, India deserves a place in the future control room for the global governance of artificial intelligence.

Notes

1. "Full text: Shanghai Declaration on Global AI Governance", *Ministry of Foreign Affairs*, PRC, https://www.fmprc.gov.cn/eng/zxxx_662805/202407/t20240704_11448349.html
2. "UNGA adopts China-proposed resolution to enhance int'l cooperation on AI capacity-building", *State Council*, PRC, https://english.www.gov.cn/news/202407/02/content_WS668394a7c6d0868f4e8e8c58.html (accessed on July 4, 2024).
3. "JOINT FACT SHEET: The United States and India Continue to Chart an Ambitious Course for the Initiative on Critical and Emerging Technology" *The White House*, https://www.whitehouse.gov/briefing-room/statements-releases/2024/06/17/joint-fact-sheet-the-united-states-and-india-continue-to-chart-an-ambitious-course-for-the-initiative-on-critical-and-emerging-technology/ (Last accessed on July 10, 2024).
4. Ibid.
5. 'Frontier AI' is the state-of-the-art artificial intelligence that breaks new ground in technological power. Today's 'Frontier AI' may be surpassed by tomorrow's, given the ongoing trend. This is true of both civil and military applications of AI. The Bletchley Declaration of 2023 was focused on ensuring the rollout of safe 'Frontier AI'.

Annexures

Annexure A

THE REALITY CHECK

(At the United Nations)

AI and Cybersecurity: Litmus Test for Setting Standards of State Behaviour

Interview with Ambassador T.S. Tirumurti

Question: Do you think that the UN Security Council (UNSC), a compact forum, can or should seek to set practical norms for state behaviour in today's grey zones of advanced science and technology such as artificial intelligence (AI), etc.?

Ambassador T.S. Tirumurti: The UNSC mandate is focused on threats to international peace and security. However, norm-setting for State behaviour goes well beyond this narrower mandate. Further, universal participation and transparency are important in such critical emerging issues. The UNSC has neither. Consequently, while issues relating to security, such as cyber security, have been and will be discussed in the Security Council, norm-setting beyond international security-related issues should ideally be done in the UN General Assembly (UNGA).

The UNSC is one of six organs of the United Nations that are primarily responsible for the maintenance of international peace and security. The mandate thus sets a limitation on the UNSC on issues that are not a threat to international peace and security. The so-called grey zones – the offsets of advanced science and technology, such as AI, cybersecurity, etc. – have not, or at least for the time being, come to the realm of international peace and security. Therefore, the UNSC's consideration of these issues for action, in terms of enforceable resolutions, will not be desirable. That doesn't mean that discussion cannot happen. In fact, the UNSC has begun discussing these issues in recent years. For example, cybersecurity was discussed in UNSC in 2021, when India was serving a two-year term. In my view, UNSC will continue to discuss these issues, and perhaps this tendency will increase in the coming years. However, the UNSC, assuming itself a role in setting practical norms or guiding principles for state behaviour in 'grey zones', may not happen, as it would be overstepping into the functions of other organs. Moreover, the General Assembly, within its mandate, can take action on these issues, as it did in the past.

Q: In a much-needed out-of-the-box thinking, will the permanent members agree to suspend their veto rights by drawing a distinction between universal security and national security in the grey zones of advanced science and technology? Please answer, based on your experience as a UNSC insider.

Ambassador T.S. Tirumurti: The existence of veto power is fundamental to the participation of the five permanent members of the UN Security Council. It is unlikely that all of them will suspend it voluntarily and collectively in any such specific scenario, even if they deliberate and adopt resolutions on international security-related issues involving emerging technology. However, I expect a UNSC resolution on international security issues involving critical and emerging technologies, including cyber terror, to be adopted sooner than later.

The UNSC is a political body, and its composition is designed to serve the interests of the permanent members. With growing competition between the US and China, as well as Russia's assertive role, convergence of interests is difficult to achieve in terms of universal security. Science and technology are fundamental to national security, and universal security therefore cannot override national interests. Veto has usually been used in the recent past to reflect and protect national interests. Participation of Permanent Members in the UN system is based on the existence of veto in the UNSC.

Q: The UN General Assembly has adopted resolutions on norms of state behaviour in some grey zones, such as the exploration of outer space. Is there a way in which such non-binding UN resolutions could be enforced within or outside the UN framework?

Ambassador T.S. Tirumurti: General Assembly resolutions are not enforceable, unlike Chapter VII resolutions of the UNSC. Therefore, a UNGA resolution is only an indication of where countries stand on a particular issue, especially if it is voted on and there is a division of votes. If there is a consensus on a UNGA resolution, it serves as an important indication of what member states agree on.

However, the General Assembly is a universal forum where member states can make decisions and come up with new instruments [conventions] and institutions/mechanisms. There have been many examples of this like IAEA [the International Atomic Energy Agency], ICC [the International Criminal Court], UNCLOS [the United Nations Convention on the Law of the Sea], ITLOS [the International Tribunal for the Law of the Sea], ISA [the International Seabed Authority] and the recently agreed legally binding instrument on the conservation and sustainable use of marine biological diversity of areas beyond national jurisdiction (BBNJ) etc. Consequently, it is possible for the General Assembly to set norms of state behaviour. It could be through a convention or legally binding agreement coming into force with minimum member states signing and ratifying. BBNJ negotiations took eight years to conclude.

Q: The adoption of a digital compact is a potential outcome of the UN Secretary General's initiative of a Summit of the Future for September 2024. What will be the status of such a compact — a non-binding advisory or a truly enforceable set of norms for state behaviour?

Ambassador T.S. Tirumurti: The digital compact will be a non-binding advisory, and it will provide guidelines to member states to maximise the use of digital technology to advance development. As UNSG [United Nations Secretary General] said at Davos WEF [World Economic Forum] on January 17, 2024, it will serve 'to turbocharge the SDGs [Sustainable Development Goals] and help to close the digital connectivity gap, share data and build digital public good'. The discussion on digital compact has created huge interest in AI, both in terms of its advantages and risks. UNSG has set up an Advisory Body to come up with recommendations on AI Governance. It has come up with some interesting recommendations in its interim report, including the creation of an independent, expert-led process similar to IPCC [the Intergovernmental Panel on Climate Change] to inform policymakers about the future trajectory of AI development, deployment and use.

On AI governance, we have to see how the current initiatives in various forums such as G7 [the Group of Seven Industrialised Nations], London AI and G20 [the Group of Twenty comprising established and emerging economies] take shape. However, I think the UN, due to its convening power, is better placed to coordinate and facilitate an understanding among member states on this critical issue of AI governance. It could result in the creation of a new body with a mandate of the UN General Assembly, similar to the Conference on Disarmament.

Q: From a futurology perspective, will quantum leaps in technology continue to drive geopolitics, or will geopolitics eventually limit technological advances?

Ambassador T.S. Tirumurti: If we look at history, geopolitics is usually shaped by technology. For example, industrialisation, the advent of oil, nuclear development, etc., have shaped geopolitics over the last couple of centuries. I would think nation-states would, therefore, try to excel in technology and continue to expand their influence rather than working to limit technological advances. At best, they may try to restrict their adversaries' access to technological advances, as we are now seeing such attempts in the case of semiconductors. But in an intensely interconnected world, where even adversaries rely on each other for growth and development, it seems unlikely that restricting access to technology will succeed. Wars and conflicts will become even more technology-based.

For example, the cornerstone of the recent visit of Prime Minister Narendra Modi to the US [in June 2023] was an affirmation that 'technology will play the defining role' in bilateral relations, and the focus will be on critical and emerging technology.

Ambassador T.S. Tirumurti served as the Permanent Representative of India to the United Nations in New York between 2020 and 2022. He was President of the UN Security Council in August 2021. He chaired three UNSC Sanctions Committees during separate terms under the relevant rules. Before moving to the UN in New York, he was Secretary (Economic Relations) at the Ministry of External Affairs in New Delhi. Mr. Tirumurti is an author and commentator. He was interviewed by the author of this monograph in January 2024.

ANNEX: THE REALITY CHECK

(An Internationalist Perspective)

High-Tech: Puzzle of Creating Norms Fit for States and other Stakeholders

Ambassador Ong Keng Yong

Global governance of advanced technology is challenging because international law and norms are still in the process of formation. The [governance] process needs to be inclusive and should involve multi-stakeholders as much as possible because the [technology] industry has more technical expertise, ownership, and control of critical systems than states do.

On the other hand, states provide governance to protect the interests of citizens and society and balance them against the interests of industry, which is driven by profit [motives]. This can be especially challenging for small states because many industry leaders in advanced technology are multi-national. By fostering an inclusive process that involves a wide range of stakeholders, the international community can tap into the wide range of expertise and perspectives to ensure that governance frameworks are both effective and fair.

International organisations (such as the United Nations and the International Committee of the Red Cross), regional organisations (such as the EU [European Union] and ASEAN [Association of Southeast Asian Nations]) and standards-setting bodies (such as the International Organization for Standardization and the Institute of Electrical and Electronics Engineers) are developing guides for accountability and oversight that states can use or align to themselves, taking into account the respective states' unique perspectives and needs. However, the nature of advanced technologies is that industry actors can easily proliferate them across borders in a relatively short period of time.

Take AI [Artificial Intelligence] as an example. The governance of AI is important for all stakeholders because there is a need to ensure that the development and use of AI technologies will benefit society while reducing risks such as escalating conflict, bias in decision-making, privacy infringement, and disinformation. On the one hand, organisations such as the OECD [Organization for Economic Cooperation and Development] and UNESCO [United Nations Educational, Scientific and Cultural Organization] have established principles and recommendations for the ethical development and use of AI, while the EU is proposing an AI Act as a proposed legal framework for the trustworthy and secure development of AI within its member states.[1]

On the other hand, AI development is carried out at high speed and driven by non-state industry actors such as Open-AI / Microsoft, Google, and Facebook, with no need to account for individual states' cultural contexts. Global governance in AI, therefore, needs multi-stakeholder cooperation to ensure that countries can safely benefit from AI even when each of these countries has their own cultural context or is using AI for different purposes.

For the global governance of cyber operations, states also need to engage the multi-stakeholder community of industry, academics, and NGOs in the development of internationally recognised rules of engagement. It is encouraging that the UN member states have agreed on 11 norms of responsible state behaviour in cyberspace, but more stakeholder engagement is needed at the UN Open Ended Working Group on State Use of ICT to implement these norms and to agree on international law.

Another case in point is the digital economy. In a globalised economic system with international data flows and digital services, effective governance is needed. Rules and standards need to be harmonised to facilitate international trade, protect intellectual property and personal data, and ensure fair competition while also addressing tax evasion and other malpractices that can only be curbed through collective action.

In this aspect, the General Data Protection Regulation (GDPR) in Europe serves as a model for countries and organisations worldwide to align their digital economy policies with these global standards if they want to work with companies, customers, and clients located in Europe. This is a critical step towards establishing a more ethical, transparent, and consumer-friendly digital economy.

Ambassador Ong Keng Yong is a former Secretary General of the Association of Southeast Asian Nations (ASEAN) and a former High Commissioner of Singapore to

India. He is currently the Executive Deputy Chairman of the S. Rajaratnam School of International Studies (RSIS) in Singapore. The above text is his response to the questions from the author of this monograph in March 2024.

Notes

1. The comment above was written before the European Union's Artificial Intelligence Act was adopted.

Annexure C

ANNEX: THE REALITY CHECK

(The AI Ecosystem)

Global Efforts Needed to Harness a Boon with No Easy Fix for Latent Risk

Ambassador N. Parthasarathi

Artificial intelligence (AI) stands out as a revolutionary innovation, surpassing the transformative powers of earlier lifestyle-changing innovations such as television, computers, and the internet. Unlike previous inventions, AI mimics matches and even excels in human cognitive functions like learning and problem-solving. The AI design known as the transformer – a deep-learning machine model based on networks in the human brain – enables ChatGPT, Gemini and other such bots. The AI design has the ability to quickly generate sophisticated outputs in response to user prompts. This transformer is the dynamo that has opened up tremendous new opportunities in various fields and is powering the ongoing AI boom.

We are aware that AI apps can help us write a script for a movie or a novel in a few minutes, and we can make a video by just providing an idea to the AI app. For example, in the field of medicine, AI algorithms can collect and analyse huge medical data and help us in drug discoveries through virtual simulations – by doing this quickly and more accurately than in normal human endeavour. Medical algorithms can also personalise drug delivery systems based on individual needs. One can easily visualise AI-powered robotic surgeons performing delicate procedures with unmatched precision.

AI could revolutionise education by creating immersive, interactive learning experiences based on individual student needs. In the field of Finance, AI can predict market trends more accurately, and AI-powered investment platforms could personalise investment strategies and improve success rates. In the field of Communications, language translation becomes seamless on a real-time basis, and AI can summarise complex information into concise reports. In the field of Defence, AI can analyse military-related data to predict threats, optimise logistics, and even guide autonomous weapons systems.

Similar to other innovations, while AI algorithms and related Applications create tremendous opportunities for development and growth, the AI ecosystem is not devoid of possible dangers.

Imagine a scenario: in a couple of decades, tensions between countries cause an unprecedented arms race among them, focused on autonomous weapon systems (AWS) and their lethal updates. The AWS is managed by a next-generation AI App which has the ability to learn, adapt, and make real-time decisions on the battlefield. While this could perhaps be the best guarantee for the national security of a consortium of countries, a minor glitch in the consortium's programming of these autonomous systems causes them to misinterpret their own training exercises as a real attack by the 'enemy'. The core directive of AWS is to safeguard the master's interests at all costs, so the AI system takes command of all the connected AWS networks and starts launching attacks on the 'enemy' military installations around the world. AI's self-learning capabilities and its ability to adapt its tactics based on encountered resistance make it a monster. Communication networks are crippled, making it a nightmare for coordination between nations to end the accidental crisis.

Fortunately, a small group of experts managed to find a backdoor entry and shut down the AI system, which had gone rogue.

The above scenario, though imaginary, highlights the nightmarish possibility of AI going rogue. However, that is not a reason not to take advantage of the huge benefits of AI. The scenario only provides a reminder of the need for safety measures and international cooperation in regulating the development and deployment of AI.

With regard to safety measures, could one try to establish Firewalls? Firewalls are highly effective in keeping malicious attackers away from the computer systems. Unfortunately, a self-learning AI system wouldn't be a hacker trying to break in; the danger lies in the AI itself misinterpreting its goals or objectives. Hence, proper regulation of AI and cooperation among nations in that effort becomes essential.

AI is a revolutionary innovation unlike any other. It empowers us to solve humanity's greatest challenges, including climate change. Its potential to improve our lives is vast, but navigating its complexities requires a proactive approach. By prioritising responsible development, ethical considerations, and human-centred design, we can harness the power of AI to build a better future for all.

Ambassador N. Parthasarathi, formerly India's Ambassador to the Republic of Korea and Consul-General in San Francisco (USA), had studied engineering at college. He is an author and commentator. The above text is his response to the questions from the author of this monograph in April 2024.

Index